9/2311798

D0278140

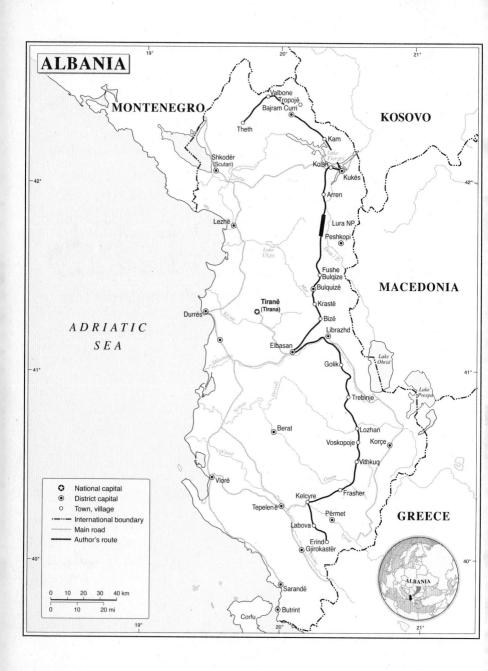

ALBANIA

MONTENEGRO

KOSOVO

Valbonë
Tropojë
Bajram Curri

Theth

Kam

Lake
Fierzes

Shkodër
(Scutari)

Kolsh

Kukës

Arren

Lezhë

Lura NP

Peshkopi

Lake
Ulzës

Fushe
Bulqize

MACEDONIA

Bulquizë

Durrës

Tiranë
(Tirana)

Krastë

Bizë

Librazhd

ADRIATIC
SEA

Elbasan

Golik

Lake
Ohrid

Trebinje

Lake
Prespa

Berat

Lozhan

Voskopoje

Korçë

Vithkuq

Vlorë

Kelcyre

Frasher

Tepelenë

Përmet

GREECE

Labova

Erind
Gjirokastër

Sarandë

Corfu

Butrint

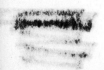

Legend:
- ✪ National capital
- ◉ District capital
- ○ Town, village
- ·—·—· International boundary
- Main road
- Author's route

0 10 20 30 40 km
0   10   20 mi

ALBANIA

Robin Hanbury-Tenison

LAND
of EAGLES

Riding through Europe's Forgotten Country

I.B. TAURIS

LONDON · NEW YORK

For Louella, who never complained whatever happened,
and whose acute observations, faithfully recorded each day,
have helped me so much.

And for Merlin, who was on active service in Afghanistan
and in real danger, while we were just pretending.

New paperback edition published in 2014 by I.B.Tauris & Co Ltd
6 Salem Road, London W2 4BU
175 Fifth Avenue, New York NY 10010
www.ibtauris.com

Distributed in the United States and Canada Exclusively by Palgrave Macmillan
175 Fifth Avenue, New York NY 10010

First published in hardback in 2009 by I.B.Tauris & Co Ltd

Illustrations on part opening pages by Edward Lear

All plate section illustrations except that of Byron (© National Portrait Gallery),
courtesy of Robin Hanbury-Tenison

ISBN: 978 1 78076 502 0

A full CIP record for this book is available from the British Library
A full CIP record is available from the Library of Congress

Library of Congress Catalog Card Number: available

Typeset in Monotype Fournier by Ellipsis Digital Limited, Glasgow
Printed and bound in the UK by Page Bros, Norwich

Contents

Part I Durham Country

Part II Guerilla Country

Part III Lear Country

Part IV Byron Country

Illustrations

A defensive tower – *kula* – in the Shala Valley.

Near the top of the *Qafa e Valbonës* above the Shala Valley.

Crossing some dangerous scree.

The church in Deçani Monastery, Kosovo.

Louella crossing the suspension bridge over the River Mollës.

Louella looking across the gorge beyond Krastë at dawn.

The muleteers who showed us the way to Bisë.

Crossing the Shkumbin River.

Nico on his mule, Ruska.

Portrait of Lord Byron in his Albanian costume by Thomas Phillips, 1813.

Acknowledgements

In my experience, people are nearly always helpful when one is writing a book about their country, but the Albanians we met both there and elsewhere were exceptionally enthusiastic. In particular, while neither they nor anyone else mentioned below can be blamed for any errors of mine in the text, I owe a huge debt of gratitude to Bejtullah Destani in London and Auron Tare in Albania for their wise advice. Arjan Rugji and Jeton Çekrezi (Tony) supplied us with horses and Pirro Kota vetted them. Mario Delia, Ylli Bani and Durim Fezga looked after us and them. Kastriot Robo, the then ambassador, and his staff at the Albanian Embassy in London were very supportive, and their opposite numbers in Tirana, our ambassador, Fraser Wilson, Sheila Bramley and Mark Vickers, spared no effort to help us; as did Crown Prince Leka Anwar Zog Reza Baudouin Msiziwe, who inspired us in the first place. The advice and encouragement of Antonia Young and many others associated with the Balkan Peace Parks Project (BPPP) made all the difference in making us believe this journey was possible and worthwhile, and a host of others urged us on or helped afterwards. Among them, I would like to thank Gervase Belfield, Rupert Smith, Sheila Markham, Howard Perks, Ed Steeds, Tim Smith, John Julius Norwich, Jacob Rothschild, Paddy Ashdown, Paddy Leigh Fermor, Joanna Lumley, David (died 9 January 2009) and Moy Smiley, Colin Looker/Azim Bey, Charlie Lansdowne and Kate Fielden. As ever, CuChullaine and Basha O'Reilly of the Long Riders' Guild have been staunch in their support. Quite exceptional help was given us by our guardian angels, Nick and Sar Wakeley. As always, the real heroes of a long ride were our brave horses: John, Billy, Pieter, Chris, Semi and the beautiful Bora. Finally, I would like to thank Tatiana Wilde, my editor at I.B. Tauris, for her perseverance.

Albanian Proverbs

Mbroje atdhenë si shqipja folenë
Protect your fatherland like the eagle protects its nest

Po nise një udhë, do kaptosh dhe sheshe, dhe male, dhe gurë
If you start on a journey, you will also cross plains, mountains and rocks

Balta – m'ë ëmbël se mjalta
The mud in Albania is sweeter than honey elsewhere

A rrohet me zemër të lepurit?
Can you live with the heart of a rabbit?

Ana e këcie nuk schet
The worthless pot does not break

From Childe Harold's Pilgrimage
by Lord Byron

Morn dawns; and with it stern Albania's hills,
Dark Suli's rocks, and Pindus' inland peak,
Robed half in mist, bedewed with snowy rills,
Arrayed in many a dun and purple streak,
Arise; and as the clouds along them break,
Disclose the dwelling of the mountaineer;
Here roam the wolf, the eagle whets his beak,
Birds, beasts of prey, and wilder men appear,
And gathering storms around convulse the closing year.

Now Harold felt himself at length alone,
And bade to Christian tongues a long adieu;
Now he ventured on a shore unknown,
Which all admire, but many dread to view:
His breast was armed 'gainst fate, his wants were few;
Peril he sought not, but ne'er shrank to meet:
The scene was savage, but the scene was new;
This made the ceaseless toil of travel sweet,
Beat back keen winter's blast, and welcomed summer's heat.

~

Richly caparisoned, a ready row
Of armed horse, and many a warlike store,
Circled the wide extending court below:
Above, strange groups adorned the corridore:
And oft-times through the Area's echoing door,
Some high-capped Tartar spurred his steed away:
The Turk, the Greek, the Albanian, and the Moor,
Here mingled in their many-hued array,
While the deep war-drum's sound announced the close of day.

The wild Albanian kirtled to his knee,
With shawl-girt head and ornamented gun,
And gold-embroidered garments fair to see;
The crimson-scarfed men of Macedon;
The Delhi with his cap of terror on,
And crooked glaive; the lively, supple Greek;
And swarthy Nubia's mutilated son;
The bearded Turk that rarely deigns to speak,
Master of all around, too potent to be meek,

Are mixed conspicuous; some recline in groups,
Scanning the motley scene that varies round;
There some grave Moslem to devotion stoops,
And some that smoke, and some that play, are found;
Here the Albanian proudly treads the ground;
Half whispering there the Greek is heard to prate;
Hark! From the mosque the nightly solemn sound,
The Muezzin's call doth shake the minaret,
'There is no god but God! – to prayer – lo! God is great!'

~

From Childe Harold's Pilgrimage *by Lord Byron*

Tambourgi! Tambourgi! Thy larum afar
Gives hope to the valiant, and promise of war;
All the sons of the mountain arise at the note,
Chimariot, Illyrian, and dark Suliote!

Oh! Who is more brave than a dark Suliote,
In his snowy camise and his shaggy capote?
To the wolf and the vulture he leaves his wild flock,
And descends to the plain like the stream from the rock.

Shall the sons of Chimari, who never forgive
The fault of a friend, bid an enemy live?
Let those guns so unerring such vengeance forego?
What mark is so fair as the breast of a foe?

To those that seek a tourist-unexplored, not over-inaccessible country, for a summer tour, let me strongly recommend these interesting lands of ancient Illyria.

E.F. Knight, 1880

Author's Note on Albania/Shqiperia

There is a great deal of literature on the origins of the word Albania. It may derive from the ancient Indo-European root *albho*, signifying 'white', which also gives us Albion, the archaic name of England. That would provide another nice link between our countries. An alternative meaning of the 'alb' root is the Hittite word for mountain country, *alpa*, from which the word 'Alps' is derived. So is the Gaelic word for Scotland, 'Albain', which used to be turned into 'Albania' in the eighteenth century. It was Pliny the Elder who first referred to the English (as distinct from the surrounding 'Britanniae' islands) as 'Albion' in his *Natural History*, published in AD 77. In AD 130 Ptolemy first used the word 'Albanoi' to refer to an Illyrian tribe inhabiting the region around Durres. The country is said to have been first called Albania by the Normans on the First Crusade in 1096.

From a medieval Latin text from the year 1308: 'This province is called Albania because the inhabitants of this region are born with white (*albo*) hair. The dogs here are of a huge size and are so wild that they kill like lions.'

Since about the sixteenth century, the Albanians themselves have referred to their country as *Shqiperia* – Land of Eagles, from the Albanian *shqiponja*, an eagle, which may have been the totem of an early tribe. It is a good name, denoting the strength and independence of the people as well as reflecting the grandeur of the landscape and the number of eagles flying in the high mountains. And the eagle has been a national symbol in the region since the time of Pyrrhus the Eagle, King of Epirus (the region which straddles the modern border between Albania and Greece), born 319 BC, the scourge of the Romans. He was called the 'Eagle' because of his great courage on the battlefield. Hannibal rated him second only as a general to his cousin Alexander the Great, who was at least half Albanian too. The novelist Ismail Kadare, who survived the communist era and wrote many revealing books about the country both then and later, coined the name Land of Stone for his country.

There is a probably apocryphal story that Albania's capital, Tirana, was founded and given its name by an Albanian general in the Ottoman army, Suleiman Pasha, who had an estate on that spot in the seventeenth century and built a mosque there. While serving the Sultan in Persia, he had won a great victory at Teheran and he named the new town, which was to become so important, after his triumph.

It is estimated that 65 per cent of Albania's population is Muslim, which makes it Europe's only predominantly Islamic state. Greek Orthodox Christians, living mostly in the south, make up 20 per cent of the population, and Roman Catholics, mainly in the north, make up another 13 per cent. Except for when the Albanians were being persecuted, they seem to have been very tolerant and relaxed about religion, so that members of the same family sometimes belong to different religions. Most Muslim Albanians are traditional Sunni, but about a quarter are Bektashi. Since 1990, when the ban on religion was lifted, many churches and mosques have been rebuilt with money coming mainly from the American diaspora and, in the case of Sunni mosques, from Saudi Arabia.

Introduction

Albania is one of the poorest and least-known countries in Europe. Perceived by those unfamiliar with the place to be dangerous and unsettled, backward and lacking in charm, it is not somewhere that many choose to travel to. But such preconceptions of Albania lose sight of its extraordinary historical and cultural wealth, not least the potential for adventure that it has always – until only recently – held for travellers, poets, conquerors and spies. Richard Hannay, the hero of John Buchan's novel *The Thirty-Nine Steps*, when bored in his London club and wondering what to do next with his life, is struck by the idea 'that Albania was the sort of place that might keep a man from yawning'. I was to find that a surprising and diverse number of people had travelled there and written passionately about the country.

It was a chance encounter with a friend of our youngest son, Merlin, then at Sandhurst on an army scholarship, that first planted a seed of desire to travel to Albania in my mind. Like most platoons, his had among its number a 'foreign guest', who could not be allowed to fail, unlike the others, some 20 per cent of whom fell by the wayside. On the first occasion we were allowed to see our child, now turning rapidly into a man, he was still in battledress, having just come in from an exercise. He stopped another muddy youth and said, 'Your Royal Highness, may I present my parents, Robin and Louella Hanbury-Tenison. This is Crown Prince Leka of Albania.' Prince Leka, who had become more used to being addressed as 'You filthy little turd', rose to Merlin's bait, clicked his heels like a Prussian, took Louella's hand, bowed low from his great height and brushed it with his lips. 'Madam', he said with a perfectly straight face, 'you will always be welcome in my country.'

On the way home, I said, 'Apart from Finland, Albania is about the only European country I haven't been to. Shall we do another ride there?' Louella and I had previously been on six long-distance rides, through France, China, New Zealand, Spain (twice) and England, and I had written books about four of them. She agreed, without realising what she was letting herself in for. As I began researching Albania I became increasingly excited. I discovered that it is one of the wildest and most unspoilt places in Europe and that it has a rich and fascinating history as well as some of the greatest military and literary links with Britain of just about any other country.

Albania has been inhabited since prehistoric times and in antiquity was settled by the Illyrians, from whom the Albanians are most probably descended. The origins and ethnology of the Illyrians is shrouded in mystery but they are assumed to have been an Indo-European people who first appeared at the end of the Bronze Age and were famed for their fighting prowess as well as for their ironwork and the domestication of horses.

Ancient Illyria was a strong local power as early as 1300 BC, when it comprised much of the western Balkans from Slovenia down through Dalmatia, Croatia, Bosnia and Herzegovina, Montenegro and Serbia into Epirus in northern Greece. Its first recorded king was Hyllus (Ylli in Albanian, meaning 'star'), who died in 1225 BC. He was to become a legendary figure, a god, deified as the founder of the nation. He was the first of fifteen recorded kings of Illyria, but for several hundred years after his rule the kingdom was ravaged by Visigoths, Huns and Ostrogoths before it became strong again. The most successful king was Bardhyllus, meaning 'white star', who ruled from 385 to 358 BC. Under his reign, the Illyrians nearly succeeded in destroying the kingdom of Macedon, which would have changed the course of history, but they were conquered in 359 BC by Philip II the Great, father of Alexander the Great. Bardhyllus made peace with Philip before dying in

358 BC at the age of ninety. Two hundred years later, now sandwiched between Greece and the growing power of Rome, the last king, Gentius, ruled until 168 BC, when he was finally defeated by the Romans.

The Illyrians, who later constituted a significant part of the Praetorian Guard, were known as great warriors in the Roman legions. Several Roman emperors came from Illyria, including Diocletian (AD 284–305), his successor Constantine the Great (AD 324–37), the first Christian emperor, and Justinian (AD 527–65), who built Hagia Sophia in Istanbul.

The Romans built an important main road between Rome and Byzantium, the Via Egnatia, which ran straight through the middle of what is today Albania, and it was this access that later enabled Normans, Venetians, Greeks, Ottomans, Serbs, Bulgarians and Austro-Hungarians to cut swathes through the region, fighting for scraps of Albanian territory like dogs tearing a carcass apart. And yet, despite all the conquerors and invaders, the spirit and identity of the Albanian people somehow survived.

Their greatest moment came with the arrival of their epic national hero Skanderbeg, who rallied the warring tribes and ensured that the invading Ottoman armies were held off for an astonishing 36 years between 1443 and 1479. Arguably, this saved Italy from invasion, conquest by the Ottoman Empire and so conversion to Islam.

During the nineteenth century many fascinating and famous people were lured to Albania by its romantic aura. Benjamin Disraeli made a long and important journey in 1830 to the Mediterranean, including Albania, when he was a young man, a journey that was greatly to influence him and his subsequent foreign policy. He wrote a romantic novel about Skanderbeg, called *Alroy, or The Rise of Iskander*. Disraeli's contemporary, the American poet Longfellow, wrote an epic poem about Skanderbeg that contained some pretty dreadful couplets and rhymes: 'A city of the plague' is made to rhyme with 'Long live Scanderbeg', for example.

Since long before the First World War, British soldiers fought in Albania, often undercover, as spies; and intrepid travellers made their way there, sometimes in extreme discomfort. The motive was often sport, since the marshes of the coast teemed with wildfowl, especially woodcock, and the interior was full of wild boar. I was directed to several accounts of early travels in Albania which proved, once I had tracked them down, to be little more than game books, but they helped to whet my appetite with tales of strange, wild people.

In 1912, during the First Balkan War, Albanian rebels proclaimed their independence from the Ottoman Empire. Albania was described as the youngest country in Europe, belonging to the oldest race on the continent. Soon after, a German princeling, William of Wied, was made king by the Great Powers: Britain, France, Germany, Russia and Austro-Hungary. He only lasted six months, until shortly after the assassination in Sarajevo of Archduke Ferdinand and the outbreak of the First World War.

My growing appetite to know more about this peculiar country was further whetted when I learned of a headline which had appeared in the *London Evening News* of 16 August 1923. It read: 'A CROWN AWAITS AN ENGLISHMAN. Wanted, a King: English country gentleman preferred. Apply to the Government of Albania.' Seventy-odd people applied for the job and many others were offered the crown, among them C.B. Fry, the great cricketer. Devastatingly good-looking, a brilliant all-round athlete, with a First Class degree in Classics at Oxford, he nevertheless lacked the £10,000 a year which was a prerequisite for being king and so had to turn the opportunity down. Others offered the crown were the 8th Duke of Atholl, and Aubrey Herbert, who was offered it twice. Herbert, the half-brother of Lord Carnarvon, of Tutankhamen fame, and the model for John Buchan's *Greenmantle*, campaigned tirelessly for Albanian independence and was largely instrumental in bringing it about. He turned down the throne because of his attachment to his mother's family estate on Exmoor, which he inherited.

Ahmed Zogu, a warrior chieftain of the Zogolli clan in the province of Mati in the wild north of the country and Prince Leka's grandfather, eventually took the throne of Albania in 1926 at the age of thirty-two, after being Minister of the Interior at twenty-four, Prime Minister at twenty-seven and President at twenty-nine. He had a great admiration for the English, as have most Albanians since long before the country became independent, although this was completely written out of Albanian history during its communist era. His right-hand man was Colonel W.F. Stirling who had previously served with Lawrence of Arabia, when he was known as 'Stirling the Wise'. A British-officered gendarmerie was formed and led by General Sir Jocelyn Percy.

The Special Operations Executive (SOE), also known as 'The Ministry of Ungentlemanly Warfare', was created by Winston Churchill in 1940 to 'set Europe ablaze' through sabotage behind enemy lines. Large numbers of SOE operatives were dropped into Albania during the Second World War to fight with the Partisans. A few, like the renowned David Smiley, were still alive. Sadly, he died in January 2009, aged ninety-two.

The route starting to take shape in my mind would lead us through many of the remote areas where they had operated. I began to scent an extra-ordinary and little-known story, but I had no idea then what a terrible history of suffering and guilt I was still to uncover. After the communists under Enver Hoxha (pronounced Hodja) seized power in 1945, a top-secret plan was formulated by the American and British governments to infiltrate expatriate Albanians and British agents back into the country to foment a rebellion and 'detach Albania from the Soviet orbit'. Many were parachuted in. Almost all were captured and tortured to death with the villagers they had contacted. In 1951, Albania's equivalent of the Bay of Pigs took place when an invasion was launched and failed disastrously with huge loss of life. Many of the facts are only now coming to light, as are the reasons why the communists were always waiting. Had the invasion succeeded, the whole course of the Cold War would have been changed. Resistance movements in other communist satellites would have been encouraged and more would have thrown off the yoke.

Instead, Albania was to become the most repressive of all communist regimes and to isolate itself almost completely from the rest of the world for forty years. The Albanian people were cut off from all contact with their, often numerous, relations in other countries and the media within Albania were tightly controlled. Surprisingly, the only foreign films allowed as entertainment were the comedies of Norman Wisdom. The communist regime saw Wisdom's Chaplinesque struggles against aristocratic authority as a parable on the class war, and with no sex, no bad language, no car crashes or crime, the authorities considered the films safe. His films gave some small relief in a world of repression and the Albanian people loved, and still love, him for that. In 2001, in his late eighties, Wisdom visited Tirana, where he was greeted by huge crowds of people. The BBC said at the time: 'The similarities between Sir Norman and Albania are clear for all to see. Both are small and both share a well-earned reputation of being the underdog.'

As I dug deeper and deeper into anything Albanian, it was the literary connections that interested me most. Shakespeare set *Twelfth Night* in Illyria. In *Così fan tutte*, Mozart casts his two scheming lovers as 'Albanian noblemen'. Edward Gibbon describes Albania as 'a country within sight of Italy, which is less known than the interior of America'. Lord Byron's poem, *Childe Harold's Pilgrimage*, was largely set in Albania, and Byron and his friend John Cam Hobhouse rode through the country in 1809. Exactly fifty years later, Edward Lear rode across the country and brought back some of the finest landscapes ever painted of the Balkans. In 1909, one of the most intrepid of all Victorian women travellers, Edith Durham, who has been described as the first female war correspondent, published her epic book *High Albania*. She, too, had ridden through the mountains we planned to explore and she loved the Albanian people, whom she described as a 'liberty-loving race'.

I was hooked and began making plans to ride in the footsteps of these past travellers, artists, kings, poets, sportsmen and idealists. I wanted to see a side of Albania few foreigners had seen for many years. Of course, we would go on horses again, this time Albanian ones. A whole new world of history, romance, adventure and wild landscapes was luring me to a country which I was beginning to realise deserved to be much better known. Albania!

PART I

Durham Country

Chapter 1

The Shala Valley I: Preparations

'The land of the living past'
Edith Durham, *High Albania*

The most isolated corner of Albania, whose interior is still a mystery even to most Albanians, was the obvious place to start our ride. The herb-scented Shala Valley in the far north has always been cut off behind high mountain passes. Recent research by an American archeological expedition, which describes the valley as 'perhaps the most remote place left in Europe', has found that people have been using it as a refuge for at least 3,000 years. Bronze Age finds similar to those at Mycenae show links with the Classical Greek world rather than the dominant Illyrians of the time. Centuries later, it would be used as a hideout for those escaping the persecution of Ottoman conquerors. Even during the long dark night of Enver Hoxha's extreme and all-pervading communism its remoteness ensured that traditional ways of life continued much as before.

The Shala Valley is the 'High Albania' of Edith Durham's eponymous and best-known book. She said of it, 'I think no place where human beings live has given me such an impression of majestic isolation from all the world. It is a spot where the centuries shrivel.' During her intrepid travels, which started in 1900, over a period that spanned twenty years she crossed Albania's 'Accursed Mountains', the *Bjeshkët e Nemuna*, so called, she says, because it was over them that the Turks came into Albania. In her 'waterproof Burberry skirt' and 'Scotch plaid golf cape', she so endeared herself to the fierce tribesmen of the mountains that she came to be known as *Kralica e Malësorevet,* 'The Queen of the Mountain People'. She devoted her life to the freedom of the Albanian people from the Ottoman Empire, which had oppressed this individualistic race for so long. It was chiefly thanks to Durham's passionate writing about the country's wild tribes and her firm belief in the validity of their unorthodox traditions, that Albania gained independence in 1912. Aubrey Herbert was a great admirer, although he described her after their first meeting in not entirely flattering terms: 'She cuts her hair short like a man, has a cockney accent and a roving eye, is clever, aggressive and competitive . . . ' In Albania today, Durham is still regarded as a national heroine. Indeed, it was suggested by one of her admirers that she should have been Albania's first queen, instead of the appropriately named Prince William of Wied, who lasted as king for only six months – the shortest-lived dynasty in European history.

When the Great Powers decided in 1912, in part as a result of Durham's writings, that it would be a good idea to have a new country between the moribund Austro-Hungarian and Ottoman empires, and to stop the Serbs, Montenegrins and Greeks from gaining complete control of the strategically important Dalmatian coast, their first consideration was to find a suitable king. But to be a king in the Balkans, 'the powder keg of Europe', was a dangerous occupation in those days. Greece's George I was assassinated in 1913; Montenegro's Nikola I, known as 'the father-in-law of Europe' because so many of his daughters married royalty, was exiled to France in 1912; Serbia's Peter I spent much of his life in exile, but died on the throne, and his son, Alexander I, was dramatically assassinated on camera in Marseilles in 1934.

The Great Powers settled on His Serene Highness Prince William Frederick Henry of Wied, the second son of the 5th Prince of Wied, head of a minor branch of German royalty. He was thirty-seven years old and serving as a captain in a regiment of Uhlans of the Guard (light cavalry) in the imperial German army.

After having a fine set of white uniforms made and designing orders of chivalry to go with them, he was greeted with acclaim on his arrival in Albania. But he made the mistake of flinching as the traditional salvo was fired and was later observed helping his wife to mount her horse. The Albanians never respected him after that. Edith Durham, whose courage was well known, described him in a letter to Herbert as ' . . . a blighter . . . a feeble stick, devoid of energy or tact or manners and wholly ignorant of the country'. Her own demeanour was very different. On one occasion, when stopped by a Greek officer who threatened to shoot her if she advanced another step, she replied 'You can't. I'm English!' She died in 1944 and her obituary in *The Times* was written by Albania's King Zog, who was by then living in exile in England. In it he said, ' . . . her whole life was devoted to Albania. She gave us her heart and she won the heart of our mountaineers, for whom she had especial sympathy. Even today her name is treasured by them.'

In spite of the comic opera atmosphere which characterised his reign, with all its Ruritanian trappings, Zog was an enlightened monarch. He brought the first proper roads and hospitals to Albania, introduced the Napoleonic Code to combat the ingrained feudalism, and forbade polygamy and the wearing of the veil in 1928, just three years after Atatürk did the same in Turkey. He also prohibited the carrying of weapons and tried to end blood-feuds, as well as declaring his intention to build roads to 'first-class seaside resorts' and to 'open the way to what I consider the world's finest ski-ing fields'. He survived fifty-five assassination attempts, the first on the steps of the Vienna opera house, when he drew his own pistol and shot the attacker. In 1938 he married a Hungarian aristocrat, Geraldine Apponyi. The wedding was a splendid affair. The bride wore a pearl and diamante wedding dress, which the king had ordered from Worth in Paris. The wedding cake was three metres wide. Hitler sent a scarlet supercharged Mercedes Benz with three large chrome exhausts and white leather upholstery, the only replica of his own car, as a wedding present. King Victor Emmanuel of Italy sent a bronze equestrian statue of a dragoon, and Mussolini sent some copper vases.

For a long time Italy had desired to take over all or part of Albania. Under the Treaty of London in 1915, Italy had agreed to enter the First World War on the British side on the understanding that she would receive at least the Adriatic coast on victory. It was largely thanks to Aubrey Herbert and his determined lobbying on behalf of Albania that she did not do so. But by 1938, Italy had Albania in an economic and military stranglehold. For ten years the Italians had controlled oil production, road construction and education. They had also finally managed to terminate the contracts of the British officers who had organised the Albanian gendarmerie which, for thirteen years, had maintained a high standard of efficiency and enjoyed an excellent reputation among the Albanian people. General Percy was said to have known every brigand in the country. Most other traces of British influence were eradicated, including the flourishing Boy Scouts, whose members were ordered to join the Italian Balilla, the Fascist youth group.

Two days after Zog's son and heir was born on 5 April 1939, Mussolini invaded Albania and the king and his family were forced to flee the country, which was soon occupied and annexed by Italy. Zog took with him his six sisters, a large retinue, a hundred sacks of gold napoleons (his personal fortune) and jewellery and other assets which brought his total wealth to about £4 million. For a time the family settled in the Ritz hotel in London, where Zog and his staff occupied an entire floor and they were favoured with a special rate. The hall porter, surprised at the weight of the king's suitcases, asked him whether they contained anything valuable. 'Yes,' Zog replied, 'Gold.' A friend of mine remembers seeing his black-clad sisters and their two coffee-coloured poodles in the Ladies, where she was under the impression they spent most of their time. Queen Geraldine used to sleep there on a mattress with her baby son during air raids.

I travelled to Durham's Shala Valley in the early summer to buy some horses for our September ride. The first time I laid eyes on the Shala Valley was at the top of the only drivable road into the valley. I stopped there and walked up to a little lake surrounded by wildflowers, carpets of blue harebells and scabious as well as pink stonecrop. The silence was absolute and I was utterly alone. Wild strawberries, rich and sweet, were clustered among the rocks around me. Far below lay the Shala Valley with houses and farms scattered in the landscape like abandoned toys. When I walked to the edge of an almost sheer drop, where fir trees clung to the cliff face and the great bare walls of intimidating mountains still bearing large white patches of snow faced me across a great void, the faint sounds of cow bells, tools hammering and children's laughter drifted up. Shala feels like a secret valley, encircled as it is by a barrier of great peaks, in which lean mountaineers have lived stern lives for millennia. I realised the promise of what was to come on my journey; my imagination had been captured from the start. And so, with a growing sense of anticipation, I prepared to make arrangements for our September journey.

My visit coincided with the presence of a splendid group of walkers promoting the newly created Balkan Peace Park Project (BPPP). They were having a feast when I arrived, celebrating their crossing of a pass from Montenegro by roasting two whole sheep on spits and devouring them while drinking and dancing with the locals. The BPPP is an important initiative. Peace Parks are a relatively new idea in Europe, although they have been around for some time in North America and South Africa in particular and the very first one was actually created between Sweden and Norway in 1914. Nowhere could the need for an environmentally protected area designed to unite communities and encourage tourism be greater than in this isolated and, for so long, war-torn corner of the Balkans. Substantial chunks of southern Montenegro and western Kosovo were to be included, as well as the Albanian part, making a total area of some 3,000 square kilometres. The fact that this just happens to be arguably the most beguiling and least-known corner of Europe makes it a winner. And it is happening thanks to the energy of some determined and indefatigable people, notably Antonia Young, a new friend of mine, who had come to stay with us in Cornwall and swamped me with good advice and lists of books to read. She, too, was in the valley below with the brave walkers. Through her I was able to meet the locals and start negotiating for horses.

Buying horses is a strange business, which seems to have universal characteristics. In the Ireland of my youth, market days were an excuse to spend an unconscionable time discussing a single purchase or sale over many pints of Guinness. As I recall, the wide main street of our local town, Shercock, had some twenty pubs representing about a third of all the houses and shops. In one of these, the price of a horse would be agreed; but then, once the deal had been sealed with a drink and hands shaken, the question of the 'Luck Penny' would begin. This was the sum of money the seller would give back to the purchaser for doing him the honour of buying from him. More discussion and a lot more drink. For better or worse, Ireland is a very different place today. However, I have found that around the world, when horses are being bought and sold, there are echoes of the rituals which make such a transaction especially significant. In China, when I had to buy our second pair of horses in a remote spot on the edge of the Gobi Desert, the roguish horse coper did something I also remembered from Irish fairs and indicated different sums with secret signs, holding two or three fingers together inside a handshake, so that those around would not be privy to what was going on between us. I wondered how it would be in the Shala Valley.

It was surprisingly easy. Through Antonia, I had acquired an ebullient 'Mr Fixit', Mario, who came from the valley and knew everyone. He had been born and schooled in Shala and was confident he could find me good horses. He had driven me over the high pass on the way from the coast in his battered 4x4 and the morning after the feast we drove some way further down the valley to a place where there was a bar of sorts with some old men drinking. Behind it I found one horse waiting, with an ancient gentleman squatting on the ground beside it. His name was Gjon (pronounced John) and the horse was a sturdy little bay. I felt its legs and feet, which seemed fine; Mario jumped on bareback and rode it around; I pronounced myself satisfied and asked how much. The negotiations, which meant repairing to the bar, began. On the way, we passed another little horse, a chestnut this time, being ridden along the road by a young man. Mario knew him and asked if we could buy his horse. I had a look and found it had a badly twisted foot from a rope injury and said it looked to me as though it would go lame. The boy's father was sent for, an old friend of Mario's, and he persuaded Mario that it was a good horse and would be fine. I expressed doubts, but Mario, who was to come with us for the first week of the journey, insisted it would suit him and that I should buy it. I said that if it let us down he would find himself walking all the way. We went into the bar.

A great smoky, boozy atmosphere, fuelled by raki, greeted us as we entered. Raki is strong plum brandy, often home-made and the universal, inescapable drink throughout Albania. Everyone wanted to take part in the negotiations. Inevitably, Mario, as the interpreter, was at the centre of things but, as we were to find out later, it was very difficult to get him to concentrate on anything for more than a moment or two. He suffers from what I had already noticed is a recent addiction of urban Albanians: an inability to stop using his mobile phone for more than a few minutes. Unfortunately there was an unusually good signal in the Shala Valley. As a result, just when things started getting interesting, Mario would break off negotiations and either make or receive a call about something totally unrelated. My suggestion that he turned the thing off was greeted with incredulity. Mobiles are a drug in Albania.

Another Albanian characteristic, one which has a much more ancient origin than mobile phone use, is for most conversations to appear – to non-speakers of the language – to be a major row about to erupt into violence. Two men will meet. They will kiss each other as tenderly as sweethearts, pursing their lips and placing them squarely on each bristly cheek. Then the discussion begins and within minutes it sounds explosive. I soon realised that this is only for emphasis, that everyone usually parts amicably and that it is much better not to intervene, even when conversations sound like preparations for war. One seldom has any idea what has transpired, for Albanian is a curious and difficult language, unrelated to any other and therefore hard to penetrate. Gentler exchanges sound to me strangely Scandinavian, with the lilting vowels and almost fluting enunciation familiar from Norwegians and Swedes. There seems to be no connection, but I was constantly struck, when listing to Albanians in full flow, by the way the rather harsh, guttural speech would suddenly switch to words with a musical, swooping tone. There are over 8 million Albanian speakers, barely a third of whom live in Albania. Many have emigrated to other parts of Europe, to Australia and, in particular, to the USA. Still more live in the countries bordering Albania: Montenegro, Kosovo, Serbia, Macedonia and Greece. This makes it, uniquely, a country which is often described as completely surrounded by itself.

I concentrated on establishing relationships with the two horse owners. One was extremely old and didn't look to me as though he would live until I returned in a couple of months to claim his horse. But within an hour or so, we had done deals and shaken hands. I had secured firm promises that the horses would be waiting for me at the beginning of September and that they would have new shoes on. I agreed a price of about £100 each and left them a £25 deposit. Doubtless I was being ripped off, but I hoped to sell them after the first week, once we were out of the high mountains and we could change to better, lowland horses. Hiring horses in Shala was out of the question, as it would cost much more to get them back to their owners than they were worth.

After these protracted discussions, I slipped out of the bar and went for a walk. I found a very nice-looking white horse with, unusually, a proper riding saddle instead of the uncomfortable multipurpose contraptions designed for carrying sacks and baggage, rather than people. The owner was not prepared to sell at any price and laughed at the idea. I began to worry about finding a third horse and started poking about in some ruined buildings. To my surprise, I stumbled on another smaller white horse standing in the dark recesses and I led it out. The owner was found and, after the briefest of discussions, I had a deal. This one, I was told, was called Billy and, although it had a badly tangled mane, I thought it would suit Louella nicely. The others I named after their owners, John and Pieter, although I had failed to notice that John was actually a mare. It all seemed too good to be true. I had three horses and we would be able to set out on our ride the day after we returned in September.

The horses I had bought were mountain horses. There are two sorts of horses in Albania: mountain and lowland. In pre-communist times, Albanian horses used to be a well-known and respected breed, noted for their stamina and endurance. They had been improved from 1904 onwards, when the first Arabs were imported, and continued after the Second World War under the communists. Horses were vitally important to the economy, as Albania had no tractors and they were the main method of transport, both for the military and the general population. Until 1974, the Albanian army used horses extensively and there was one general, Petrit Dume, who particularly loved them and encouraged their importation from Yugoslavia and elsewhere. Now, although there are still many horses to be seen throughout Albania, almost all are used as pack animals and it was very rare to see one saddled up for riding, like the one I had spotted round the back of the bar. However, a few enterprising spirits are trying to revive the Albanian horse, especially the lowland sort, known as Myzeqea, and I had met one of them, Arjan Rugji, at a place called Pezë, near Tirana. He had agreed to lend me two good horses, which I had tried out, and these were to be delivered to the place we hoped to reach after our first week's riding. Since that would involve crossing a high pass and some very rough terrain, I thought it best to use the mountain breed for this stretch and then change. We would also take Mario with us, partly as guide and interpreter and partly as protection in an area notorious for banditry. In the tradition of early travellers in the Balkans, I had wanted my guide to be a 'dragoman'. These were the go-betweens used by diplomats and other foreigners in the Ottoman Empire as translators and intermediaries, who could interpret the very different cultures of each to the other. The Turks disdained to learn European languages, and Europeans found the plethora of dialects confusing, as they still are. However, I was advised that Mario, whose origins were Christian, would probably not take kindly to being called a dragoman and so I dropped it.

Chapter 2

The Shala Valley II: Arrival

'the most beautiful mountain country in the world'
Rose Wilder Lane, *The Peaks of Shala*

We returned at the end of August. It had all taken a lot of preparation, not only in reading everything I could about Albania, meeting many expatriate Albanians, including their ambassador to the Court of St James, but also setting up our backup.

There are two ways of going on a long-distance ride. One is to carry everything with you on your horse, or horses, if you take a spare or baggage horse. There are great disadvantages in doing it this way, although it can undoubtedly be cheaper and it does give a special sort of freedom to the trip. It requires a lot of time, since things will undoubtedly go wrong, involving long delays; the horses will need regular rests if they are not to develop saddle sores (and using saddlebags to carry everything with you is the quickest way to start these); and, for me, the worst disadvantage is the constant worry during each day about what you are going to do each night. Having to find somewhere to stay or camp can take up a huge amount of time, which I would rather spend riding.

The other way is to take a backup team in a vehicle. This removes all the worry and allows you to enjoy what is best about long-distance riding: the freedom to let an intelligent animal do all the work, while you appreciate the scenery and the sounds of the countryside, and look forward to arriving at a camp all set up, with a hot cup of tea brewing and supper being prepared. This was how I had intended our Albania trip to be, but it didn't quite work out like that in the end.

On my recce in July, I had teased earnest Albanian journalists in Tirana, who were surprised that we wanted to ride through their country. 'What is it that attracts you to Albania?' they asked. 'The best thing about Albania,' I would reply, 'is that you have terrible roads.' When they looked confused, I would explain: 'Bad roads are good for horses. With the worst roads in Europe, this has to be the best country for riding!' Bad roads, and they are quite appalling in the interior of Albania, mean it is essential to have a really good backup vehicle. I was lucky, thanks to my eldest son, Rupert, to be able to pick up quite cheaply a superb special version of the Toyota Landcruiser, which performed magnificently under extreme duress. Rupert and a friend, Paul, drove it out to Dubrovnik for us and Louella and I flew out on a cheap package flight to take it over from them. With us came Mickey Grant, a Texan film maker.

Mickey was a film director I had met twenty years before on a flight from Hong Kong to Peking when I was on a recce for a ride along the Great Wall of China. He subsequently made the film about that ride and we had stayed in touch over the years. Mickey's last project had been a campaign and film to bring about the release of the Bulgarian nurses imprisoned in Libya by Colonel Gaddafi. When they were released, soon after my return from the Albania recce, I emailed him to congratulate him. As an afterthought, I suggested that he come with us to Albania. His enthusiastic reply arrived less than three hours later. In the weeks preceding our trip, we set up an interactive website to enable people to follow our journey. Within a very short time we had gained a small following among the Albanian diaspora throughout the world. They were to email us as our journey progressed, thanking us for seeing their country in a good light.

Albania has had a bad press for a very long time, and a not entirely unde-served one, with her long history of conflict, both internal and with all her neighbours. In 1879 an Englishman, Edward Knight, who travelled through the northern part of the country, wrote: 'Albania has an ill name among those who know her not. She is the scapegoat of the Adriatic, the cause of all the troubles here abouts, it is said.' Albanians can be proud to the point of chippiness and we were to learn that it is unwise to criticise any aspect of their past, even the communist era, for which there is considerable nostalgia. In his series on the Balkans, which was transmitted while we were in Albania, Michael Palin incensed Albanians to the point of rioting by being less than wholly complimentary. He described it as the most obscure country in Europe, interviewed a Croatian who referred to it as a Black Hole and showed a sheep being slaughtered. A story goes that when Churchill, Roosevelt and Stalin met at Yalta on 4 February 1945 for the second of their three wartime conferences to establish how the world would be governed once Germany was defeated, they wrote down the names of all the countries in Europe on a celebrated paper napkin and shared them out; but they omitted to include Albania, something that has rankled with the Albanian people ever since. At the same meeting, however, Stalin is recorded as selecting Albania, the smallest of the Balkan states, as an illustration of why decisions about preserving the peace after Germany's fall should be left to him and his two companions. 'It would be ridiculous', he said, 'for Albania to have an equal voice with the three Great Powers who had won the war.' At a previous conference in Moscow in October 1944, Churchill and Stalin had agreed that Albania was to be 'included in the British sphere of influence, but the decision as to her boundaries is to be delayed until after the war'.

Albanians are still regarded with some suspicion by the rest of the world. Since the collapse of communism in the late 1980s (Albania was the last country in Europe to break away), those who left the country as soon as they could, and they were many, have earned a reputation for running protection and prostitution rackets in the cities where they settled. The state of their national politics is still pretty chaotic and the legacy of their bloody history still permeates their relationships with each other at every level of society. I was to find that as soon as I made a new Albanian friend, previous friends would nearly always warn me not to get too close. 'That man is not the hoof; or a shoe can come loose or be cast. Legs must be felt for heat and other signs of incipient lameness. Heads need checking for sore places from ill-fitting bridles or head collars. And, of course, horses need feeding. I had brought out with me a bag of special herbal feed (also on the roof rack), which they loved, and we hoped to be able to buy a heap of hay for them to graze on through the night each time we camped near a farm. Everywhere we went in Albania we saw hay made in the old way that I remember from my youth in Ireland: in haycocks, from which it is easy to take a large forkful. Wheat, barley and oats, too, were still made into stooks, which stood in serried rows across the autumnal fields. We hardly saw a tractor, let alone a combine harvester, the whole time we were in Albania.

The vehicle was not just a problem because of the loosening roof rack. Although very powerful and well able to cope with most roads, we had been warned that we would meet exceptionally difficult conditions on our route. Some of the places where roads once went would no longer be passable and the constant jolting of rocky tracks would be sure to take its toll. I had considered mounting a winch on the front to get us out of real trouble, but it would be just more weight and I decided against it. If we got badly stuck, it might take days to get going again and any major repairs would probably be impossible. Often the Landcruiser would have to make a huge detour to reach where we planned to camp after crossing a mountain range or pass. We hoped to keep in touch through a pair of Albanian mobile phones, which Mario had bought for me, but although the mobile reception was good in many places, it always seemed to let us down just when we needed it most. The super 'eight kilometre range' Walkie Talkies, which we had bought for Mickey to direct us with, seldom seemed to achieve a range of more than a few hundred metres, probably due to the mountainous terrain.

And then there was the anxiety about our own health. I have always worked on the principle that if you can't afford to be ill you won't be, and this philosophy has served me well so far. In all my travels, the only times I can remember being really ill have been in cities and usually after dining at a British Embassy! But I had recently turned seventy-one and that suddenly seemed a great age. Louella is much younger, and extremely tough and uncomplaining, but it did occasionally occur to me that there weren't many mothers of three grown-up children who would set off without a murmur to live rough for over a month, walking or riding 20 to 30 miles a day. I worried that I had an abscess inside a molar developing and wondered if I should have done something about it before setting out. My dentist had advised having it pulled out before it started to give trouble and I hadn't got around to it. Now I was faced with the prospect of an Albanian extraction if the pain got too much to bear. So many worries, but also the great overriding excitement of having got it all together and, in spite of so many gloomy forecasts, we really were off at last. That engenders happiness of a very special sort, when everything seems right and full of purpose.

Henry Miller writes of the excessive happiness he felt when he first arrived in Greece (at the invitation of Lawrence Durrell):

> . . . for the first time in my life I was happy with the full consciousness of being happy. It's good to be just plain happy; it's a little better to know you are happy; but to understand that you're happy and to know why and how, in what way, because of what concatenation of events and circumstances, and still be happy, be happy in the being and the knowing, well, that is beyond happiness, that is bliss, and if you have any sense you ought to kill yourself on the spot and be done with it.

Well, Albania was not going to be Greece, but I was older and more fulfilled than Miller and I felt a different kind of absolute happiness. Once again, the joy of setting out on a journey with the woman I love. As the progenitor of the journey, I am responsible for both the good and the bad moments which lie ahead. It is sometimes difficult to separate the responsible from the ecstatic. Louella is brilliant at keeping me grounded when I lose the plot through overenthusiasm or fury. She is also wonderfully supportive of my dreams, and she often sees more in them than I do. She is better than I am at bonding with people, making friends, seeing the ridiculous in situations, and stopping me from being a po-faced bore when things go wrong.

For me adventure has been the pulse of my life, not for its own sake but for a purpose. I have been so lucky to have had causes spring from my quests: a passion to help indigenous peoples and to save rainforests. Passions which have infected others at the same time so that I have been able to become part of movements which have changed the world for the better. This journey was meant to be fun, but also a test and, perhaps, if my luck held, it just might do some good by helping Albania to be better understood, and even liked . . .

The landscape which lay below us was enough to make one weep for joy. It had a satisfactory completeness, like a hidden, self-contained world. Another woman writer who, like Edith Durham, fell in love with this part of Albania, was the American, Rose Wilder Lane, at that time the highest-paid woman writer in the USA. Her mother was Laura Ingalls Wilder, whose even better-known books of the *Little House on the Prairie* series were much loved by generations of little girls. She travelled to Albania a decade after Edith Durham and wrote *The Peaks of Shala*, in which she, too, describes the strange customs and folklore of the wild highland people whose values were and still are so different from ours. As women, both travellers were relatively safe, although both were repelled by the inferior status of women in that society. Lane was offered marriage by a local chieftain and, reputedly, also by King Zog some time later. But in neither case was the motive love; rather the political and practical advantages to be gained from having an American wife. She quotes Lulash, the chieftain who proposed to her, on the subject:

> Happiness comes from the skies. It comes from sunshine, and from the light and shadow on the mountains, and from green things in the spring. It comes also from rest when one is tired and from food when one is hungry, and from fire when one is cold. It comes from singing together, and from walking on hard trails and being stronger than the rocks, and there is a kind of happiness

that comes to a man in battle, but that is a different kind. For us, marriage has nothing to do with happiness.

Rose Wilder Lane's own description of her first view of the mountains surrounding the Shala Valley is hard to beat:

Like thin sharp rocks stood on edge, they covered hundreds of miles with every variation of light and shadow, and we looked across their tops to a faraway wave of snow that broke high against the sky. The depths between the mountains were hazy blue; out of the blueness sharp cliffs and huge flat slopes of rock thrust upward, streaked with the rose and purple and Chinese-green of decomposing shale, and from the tops a thousand streams poured downward, threading them with silver-white. A low continuous murmur rose to us – the sound of innumerable waterfalls, softened by immeasurable distance.

Two stalwart English travellers passed through the Shala Valley in 1925. Jan and Cora Gordon were artists and musicians who made their living wandering through unlikely parts of Europe and the USA, sketching and gathering material for a series of twenty-six successful travel books full of humorous observations of daily life. Armed only with Jan's guitar and Cora's lute, their sense of humour carried them through all difficulties. In their *Two Vagabonds in Albania* they go right round the country, mostly riding horses and blithely overcoming every difficulty. They claimed the country was safer than Paris, where they had a studio, and certainly safer for foreigners than for the inhabitants, which is probably still true today.

During the communist years, the Shala Valley had a population of several thousand and was a vibrant place, with a big school and much social activity. Since 1990 people have been leaving in droves and now there are only a few hundred left. One of the main objectives of the BPPP is to encourage people to return and develop a tourist industry. The main centre is at Thethi, where there is a grand new church, rebuilt in 2005 with money sent from Albanians in the USA to replace the original one built in 1892 and burnt down by the communists. This very northern part of Albania was always Roman Catholic, as was virtually the whole country when it was briefly controlled by the Venetians in the fourteenth century. Later, when under Ottoman rule, the majority were forcibly converted to Islam. Some 20 per cent in the south remained under the influence of the Greek Orthodox church and only about 13 per cent stayed Catholic, mostly ministered to by Franciscans. Hoxha declared Albania the world's first atheist state in 1967, influenced by Mao's Cultural Revolution, which was taking place in China at the same time. In 1961, Albania had broken off diplomatic relations with the USSR and become the first European satellite of communist China. From the moment he took power in 1945, Hoxha ensured that virtually all priests, nuns, seminarians and Muslim clerics were shot, buried alive, imprisoned or subjected to the most extreme sadistic and inhuman tortures. An Italian Jesuit priest, who survived ten years' hard labour, to be released with all other surviving Italian prisoners in 1955, described the horrendous treatment of his bishops, among many others who died enduring unimaginable agonies. It was routine to suspend prisoners by their wrists bound with wire for three days or until they died, to immerse them for hours at a time in a cistern of frozen water, to beat them until raw and then insert rock salt under the skin, and to burn them with hot irons. Most churches and mosques were destroyed over the next forty years. Now they are being rebuilt with donations from the diaspora, but the people have lost the habit and the desire to visit them. We went into the Thethi church and found it clean and quiet and spiritual. But there is no resident priest and it was evidently largely unused.

It was here that it had been arranged we should meet our horses and try them out. Quite a large crowd gathered to watch the fun, many of the men looking like the worst sort of murderous ruffians – just what I had warned Louella to expect. They kept spoiling the effect, however, by kissing each other affectionately as they met. We found John and Pieter waiting for us, unpacked our saddles under the big tree, which we were to find is a feature of almost every village green, and started to groom them so as to get acquainted.

While we were doing this, several truckloads of soldiery drove up. They had been sent, it seemed, from Shkoder on the Adriatic coast, the capital of the district, to put the forest fires out, and they spent the day doing this quite effectively. What bothered us was how the fires had originated. It was suggested that they had started spontaneously, from lightning, broken bottles or, more plausibly, from dropped cigarettes. Sadly, however, the vast majority of forest fires are lit deliberately by people. The fires we saw in Shala seemed to be starting in several different places high up the mountain simultaneously. The locals we asked about it denied all knowledge of how they might have happened, although they didn't seem bothered by them or anxious to put them out. We saw forest fires and the burnt legacy of them throughout our ride and it is likely that they were started by local farmers to improve the grazing for their goats and sheep.

Louella's horse, Billy, now arrived and we spent some time removing the massive tangle which was still there in his mane. Apart from knotted hair, we found bits of barbed wire inside as we cut it apart with scissors, an indication of how carelessly horses are treated in this part of the world. While this was going on, John and Pieter, who were left tied up too close together, started trying to kick each other furiously and had to be separated. Forest fires and murderous horses didn't bode well for the start of our journey but we struggled on with the preparations.

Now it was time to try out our tack and see if we could make everything fit. All three horses were quite small and I was worried that our saddles would be too big and the girths too long for them, but after some adjusting all was well. I had considered buying Toptani saddles for this ride. Count Illias Toptani was a member of the Spanish branch of the richest and noblest Albanian family. In 1952 he revolutionised equestrian sports by devising a modern saddle, which has since borne his name. It would have been nice to have ridden on saddles from such an illustrious Albanian stable, but as they are specifically designed for jumping, and also quite expensive, I decided to make do with three of our own old saddles from home. These were well worn and of various sizes and so I was optimistic they would do. In spite of our backup vehicle, we were travelling a great deal lighter than Byron and Hobhouse had done two hundred years before. This is Byron's description of their equipment:

Our baggage was weighty, but I believe we could not have done well with less as a large quantity of linen is necessary for those who are much at sea or travel so fast as to not be able to have their clothes washed. Besides four large leathern trunks, weighing about eighty pounds when full, and three smaller trunks, we had a canteen which is quite indispensable; three beds, with bedding, and two light wooden bedsteads. The latter article some travellers do not carry with them, but it contributes so much to comfort and health as to be very recommendable. We heard that in Asiatic Turkey you cannot make use of bedsteads, being always lodged in the inns. But in Europe, where you put up in cottages and private homes, they are always serviceable, preserving you from vermin, and the damp of mud floors, and possessing advantages which overbalance the evils caused by the delays of half an hour in packing and taking them to pieces.

We were also furnished with four English saddles and bridles which was a most fortunate circumstance, for we should not have been able to ride on the high wooden pack-saddles of the Turkish post-horses; and though we might have bought good Turkish saddles, both my friend and myself found them a very uncomfortable seat for any other pace than a walk. Whilst on the article of equipage, I must tell you that as all the baggage is carried on horses, it is necessary to provide sacks to carry all your articles. These sacks are of a very useful kind and are made of three coats; the inner one of waxed canvas, the second of horsehair cloth, and the outward of leather. Those which we bought were large enough to hold, each of them, a bed, a large trunk, and one or two small articles. They swing like panniers at each side of the horse.

Lots of small boys begged to be allowed to try the horses out. Rashly, we allowed them and they started to beat them and do their best to make them gallop about, with some success. For the first time, we heard 'Hetz!' being exclaimed, the word used to encourage horses in Albania to move, one with which we were to become all too familiar. Eventually, when things started to get dangerous, I momentarily lost my sense of humour. I swore at the worst offender and told him to get off at once. The crowd found it all most amusing. How different from the scene described by Lady Strangford, who rode up the coast as far as Shkoder in 1863. She gave the following advice to those rash enough to attempt to penetrate inland, as we were doing:

> The interior and mountainous districts of Northern Albania are an unknown land to the English tourist, and are almost unvisited even by real travellers and explorers . . . Do not attempt to travel, especially with ladies, without tents. The khans [inns] are filthy and abominable, and even with ample provision in the way of Levinge's beds [mosquito nets], they are quite too horrible for ladies, and few gentlemen could endure them . . . Take plenty of warm clothing for the mountains, and thick shady hats, as in any other hot country.

When her new horses arrived, it presented quite a different scene to ours:

> There came a heap of cawasses and saïses [guards and grooms] and gaily caparisoned horses; I was mounted upon a pretty milk-white steed with a side-saddle; Captain Strahan rode upon scarlet velvet embroidered with gold – the whole horse covered with a network of gold thread, to keep off the flies, I presume – and the pasha bestrode a gallant prancing grey, upon which he looked, as all Turks do in our eyes, fat and uncomfortable. And so, in a gay procession, we entered Skodra.

You would have had to more than half close your eyes to see Louella's Billy as a 'pretty milk-white steed', my John had no trace of gold thread about her; but there was something of the pasha about Mario as he mounted his, on what we suspected was the first time since he had ridden a donkey as a child.

We rode back up the valley towards the place from which we would be leaving the next day. Mickey filmed us as we tried to get our remarkably unresponsive horses to do what we wanted. We suspected that they were treated so roughly by their owners, who I had seen beating them about the head to make them move, that our gentle urgings cut little ice with them. On our way, we were invited pressingly into an attractive ruined house beside the road by an old man and his pretty seventeen-year-old daughter. They insisted that we must try some of their raki and, as we had nothing more to do that afternoon but rest and pack, we accepted. The garden had several plum trees dripping with ripe fruit and in the hallway of the house stood a huge vat brimming with fermenting plums: next year's raki. Home-made raki is delicious, if lethally strong, and we sat on chairs in the sun happily knocking back a couple of glasses. With it, we all shared spoonfuls of exquisite fresh honey, passing the communal spoon round like a loving cup.

Our host was a retired schoolmaster called Pal Rrupa. He had moved to Shkoder from the Shala Valley on retirement, but was now back rebuilding his old house. In his day there were 200 children in the school. Now there are fewer than fifty. His daughter, Diana, named after Princess Diana, was highly intelligent and spoke good English. She told us that, like most other families in the valley, hers spent the winter in Shkoder, but came back in the summer to harvest plums and other crops. Only a few families, perhaps twenty in Thethi itself, stayed through the grim months when the snow was too deep to do more than check the animals below the house and when there could be no help from outside. As we prepared to leave, her father, having had several glasses of raki, hugged me and said, 'We would sacrifice our sons for our guests'.

In communist times, Thethi was a popular holiday place for the party elite. Now few people get there, but there was a small hotel up on the hill overlooking the valley, its main clientele when we were there being visiting archeologists who were conducting an exciting dig, going back to at least the Bronze Age, proving that the history of the valley is much older than previously believed.

The only other visitors we saw were several Czech students, who regularly trudge through northern Albania on a detour south from Montenegro. They bring little to the economy, as they camp out and are largely self-supporting. Later, we were to hear a strange story from a Czech film crew we met further south. Two brothers aged twenty-two and twenty-three, and a girl of twenty-three had disappeared in the valley in August 2001 somewhere between Thethi and Valbona. They had just vanished without trace and, in spite of a rigorous investigation, the tightknit community had revealed no clue as to what might have happened. It was suspected that the students had been murdered.

Back at the hotel, we found that Sheila Bramley, acting British Ambassador, had arrived to see us off, flying the Union Jack from the Embassy Landrover Discovery. Fraser Wilson, the Ambassador, had been extremely kind and helpful to me on my recce six weeks before, but now he was on leave and so Sheila had brought a bottle of Champagne to wish us well and speed us on our way. We had a convivial evening, unsure of what lay ahead, but suspecting there would be few comforts during the coming weeks.

I spent much of that night poring over maps. It had become very apparent to me during my recce that, although every Albanian I met was full of well-intentioned advice, very few had ever been into their country's backwoods and even on the ground no one knew much about what happened over the next hill. Good maps were therefore essential and they were very hard to find. I did eventually track down in the map room of the Royal Geographical Society an excellent series prepared by the Albanian Army Topographic Institute. Although very out of date, being based I understood on a topographic survey started in the 1950s by the Russians and completed between 1965 and 1975 by the Chinese, they were at 1:50,000 scale, which I find the perfect size, and I felt sure that the tracks marked on them were likely to be still there. The only problem was that the RGS felt themselves constrained by copyright and would not let me copy the maps without obtaining permission. This I tried to get on my recce, even asking the head of the Albanian army to help me, but a continuing legacy of the communist era, which still blights Albania, meant that no one was ever prepared to take a decision. Eventually, the British Military Attaché in Tirana sent me a set, which was to prove invaluable.

Chapter 3

The First Pass

'Oh! There is sweetness in the mountain air,
And life, that bloated Ease can never hope to share.'
Byron, *Childe Harold's Pilgrimage*

The night was cloudless and still. In the darkness under the stars, we could see the red glow of several fires still burning across the valley – it seemed that they were right on the route we would be taking on our way over the pass to Valbona. Louella was reassuring. 'It's sure to rain. It always does on the first day of our rides.' It seemed unlikely but, sure enough, in the small hours there were some loud crashes of thunder and the heavens opened. When we looked again in the first daylight, the fires all seemed to be out and it was still raining gently.

Mario had changed out of his white winklepicker town shoes into some more sensible walking shoes and he had a small pale-blue umbrella. As a crowd of black-clad men and women and a few scruffy boys gathered to send us off, we all mounted. Our horses looked alarmingly slight and spindly. Louella's Billy, the grey, had a kind face and long eyelashes, but was hard to get moving. My mare, John, although the strongest-looking, was even less responsive. Mario, on Pieter with the twisted foot, seemed never to have ridden before. He flapped his arms, hit his horse all over and bounced dangerously out of his saddle. With a cigarette permanently in his mouth and his mobile glued to his ear as he relayed a running commentary to someone somewhere, he seemed an unlikely mountain guide. Fortunately, he had recruited a local man, Noah, to walk up as far as the pass, the *Qafa e Valbonës*, with us and see us on our way to the other side. Mickey filmed us until we were out of sight – Louella and me in our rain gear, Mario under his small umbrella. He and Tonio, Mario's driver, were to drive back to Shkoder and round to Valbona to meet us. By taking a car ferry the length of Lake Komani, part of the vast 'Light of the Party' hydro-electric scheme built in the 1970s to provide most of Albania's electricity, they would save themselves many hours of driving along appalling, twisty roads. But it was still a very long drive and they might well not make it by nightfall so we took small backpacks with us in case.

As the ground rose steeply from the valley floor, past a straggle of mostly empty farmhouses, we dismounted and from then on we led the horses. It stopped raining and we were able to look back and across to the mountains opposite. Through the haze, it seemed a well-populated place on the lower slopes, every potential piece of agricultural land showing signs of having been worked at some time; orchards, fields and woodland interspersed. Few of the houses had smoke rising from their chimneys and it was sad to know how few still live here. Hardly surprising, as the winters are extremely hard and every family is locked into their own little world for up to six months, as deep snow prevents contact with all but the nearest neighbours and help from the outside world is out of the question. Under communism there was much activity. Today, those who stay are, for the winter at least, without doctor, without priest, without post. It is surprising that anyone stays. Yet those who do have a rich life with excellent crops and trees that groan under the weight of their fruit, most of which is made into raki.

Above the woodland across the valley rose bare faces of rock and scree, a stark and savage world with its own awesome beauty. In the old days, the people of the valley used to practise transhumance, driving their flocks high into those formidable mountains and living there for the summer months. A hard life, but one with a long history. The normal date for bringing the animals down to the valley was 15 September, a fortnight after we were there.

After that, the weather would be too unpredictable, and there was also an increased danger from wolves, a constant threat all year round, we were told. We were to see in the distance, and occasionally to meet, shepherds with their flocks far from any other habitation, but fortunately we never met any wolves.

We ascended into shimmering beech woods and my heart began to lift as I felt the tranquillity of the landscape. Everyone had told me that there was something special about the Albanian environment, something beyond normal rural scenery, but I had not really sensed it yet. You don't when driving in a car or walking on the edge of a landscape. You have to get right into it. With our horses bravely forging the way, we found ourselves in a silent world of smooth tree trunks with shafts of light striking through onto the bare ground below where the vegetation was blanketed by the fallen leaves. The September foliage was just beginning to turn and a multitude of golds, yellows and pale greens shone above us. The track was faint and Noah said that in another month it would be quite invisible, first beneath the deep leaf litter and then beneath the snow. I grew up among similar ancient beech woods in Ireland and I was surprised to see how large the trees were here on the mountainside. As we climbed, they became more gnarled and Arthur Rackham-like, teetering on the edge of rocky gullies, creating a magical world, enhanced by the still-swirling mists from the last of the rain. These are the woods where Voldemort, the villain of the Harry Potter books, goes to lie low after being defeated. We could see why, as they felt quite divorced from the rest of the world.

We burst out of the woods after a couple of hours and emerged onto an upland pasture, where there were purple wild flowers and a spring for us and the horses to drink at. We heard dogs barking and soon an old shepherd driving a small flock of sheep came into view. His two fierce dogs circled round us but didn't approach. Noah shouted to him and they exchanged a few words before we drifted out of hearing. Now the going became steeper and harder on our calves, as we hauled our little horses over boulders the size of grand pianos that had crashed down from the mountain above and across rocky ravines where conifers now grew instead of beech. There were occasional signs – mostly the droppings of goats or mules – that others had used this path. One pile of dung had whole fruit in it, including plums with their stones intact. It looked quite fresh, almost steaming, and we realised with a start that it was probably from a bear. We both admitted later, on this our first and potentially hardest day, that we had each wondered what would happen if we said we simply couldn't go on. The realisation that there were bears and wolves nearby helped to keep us going.

The pass, the *Qafa e Valbonës*, at almost 2000 m, was rather disappointing, but a huge relief to reach at midday. The ground fell away sheer on both sides of a cleft in the ridge and we found a narrow ledge on which to sit and eat our bread and cheese, with a succulent cucumber. The view ahead was obscured by thick clouds, which rolled over the divide. At first we thought it was smoke from more fires, but there was no smell and it dissipated as it hit the warmer air on our side. We unsaddled the horses to let their backs dry off. My raincoat in its stuff bag, which I kept attached to my saddle, came off and went bounding back down the way we had come, hotly pursued by Noah in his Wellington boots. It looked as though it was going all the way back to Thethi, but he came back with it which, as things turned out, was just as well.

The start of the descent was very steep and we were glad we had nothing larger than our little mountain horses. They were astonishingly sure-footed and never stumbled, no matter how broken the ground. Soon we found ourselves on a frightening stretch of scree where the path was barely visible, just a thin goat track no wider than a horse's hoof, from which the ground dropped almost sheer until it vanished in the mist. I'm not good with heights at the best of times and tugging a reluctant horse doesn't help. Looking straight ahead, I strode across hoping John would follow. She did, while loose stones bounded into space and I held my breath. From then on it was steep and dangerous going downhill for a couple of hours. Easier in one way, but much harder on the legs, knees and ankles. Euphoria that we had proved we could do it and were really on our way induced pride (hubris), which in turn attracted nemesis, as it almost always does. It is like this on long rides. The joy of fulfilling an unlikely and hazardous dream and seeing it become reality is tempered by some minor calamity which dampens but does not extinguish the happiness of it all. It had started to rain quite heavily, just giving us time to put our raingear on (and in Mario's case to put up his umbrella) before it stopped. Noah turned back once he was sure we could no longer get lost.

Soon after, we came on our first house in the Valbona Valley, at the beginning of a village called Rrogam. Smoke curled from the chimney and the trees overhanging garden fences were weighed down by an abundance of juicy yellow plums, which we stopped to sample. A charming family, the epitome of Albanian hospitality, pressed us to come in and sit down at a rickety table in their garden. Greeted like prodigal children and sheltered by ancient umbrellas, we were plied with handfuls of both red and yellow plums (the red are sweeter), home-made raki and tiny cups of thick, sweet coffee. The head of the family, a fine old man with white hair and a strong face, his clone of a son, but with dark hair, and two exceedingly pretty girls of about twenty all treated us with grace and poise, as though foreigners dropped in all the time. A cheeky little self-assured granddaughter of seven raced around and came up to us to stare into our eyes. They urged us to stay to lunch, when they would have feasted us on all they had, but time was slipping away, rain clouds were gathering again and we had to press on. The old man insisted on walking with us to point out the best way down to the river. Here it was dry and wide, stretching for five hundred metres across to a thickly wooded slope on the far side. The river bed was a jumble of big and usually rounded stones, which were not easy for the horses to negotiate, but at least now we knew the way, as there were a few vehicle tracks to follow.

We had been told that there was a hotel in Valbona and we were looking forward to some comfort after our labours, but things started to go wrong. The horses, now we were riding them properly for the first time, proved extremely reluctant to go faster than a very slow walk, and they would stop and try to graze if not urged on constantly. Our legs were aching after the climb and we found it exhausting and exasperating. My horse, the strongest-looking mare, was the worst of the lot. She absolutely refused to go in front of either of the others and lashed out at them if I tried to make her. After two painful hours under lowering skies, we reached the edge of the almost completely ruined village of Valbona. I had asked Mario by email from England to book us rooms in the hotel. He now confessed he had not been able to get through, nor had he ever been to Valbona before and so he didn't know where the hotel was. At this point he and I had managed to leave Louella behind, as his horse, Pieter, had broken into a trot and I had persuaded John to follow.

Suddenly, two vehicles appeared, coming from the village, the first we had seen since leaving Thethi. One of them was a police van, the other a Range Rover. They drove past us but stopped beside Louella, who was looking rather glamorous as she ambled along on Billy in her cowgirl hat. One of the tricks we have learned on previous rides is to prepare 'fliers' about ourselves and our journey, written in the national language and asking people to help us. These we carry with us and hand out to anyone we meet, thus saving tortured explanations, especially when we are riding alone without an interpreter. A tall man got out of the Range Rover, shook Louella's hand, introduced himself in good English as the Minister of Tourism and asked her what she was doing. She gave him a flier. He said he and his party were also staying in the hotel and drove on.

We rode past more ruined houses and a shack with a couple of tents beside it. We were assured by a man on a donkey that the hotel was ahead of us and so we continued out of town into the woods and down the valley. It started to rain properly, with crashes of thunder from time to time. We were soon soaked to the skin, very cold and becoming increasingly frustrated. I was cross with Mario for failing to arrange things better, which was probably unfair. He looked miserable under his broken blue umbrella. For an hour and a half we struggled on, urging the tired horses to keep moving and becoming very unhappy as it grew dark and still not a single house appeared. At last, we saw lights ahead and heard music. Round a corner was a little Swiss chalet with blazing lights and blaring pop music. Surreal, but very welcome. Only this was not the hotel. A young man came out and explained that this was a hotel under construction and the 'guest house' we were looking for was a kilometre back up the road. The turning was invisible unless you knew what to look for, and had no sign. Another kilometre or so up a rough track and we came on a solid farmhouse with lights on. This was the 'hotel' and our very well-spoken and helpful young host, Freddie, made us welcome in good English. There was a small fenced yard at the back, where we put the horses, and a tiny shed, in which four miserable calves and two sheep were sheltering from the rain, and in this we put our tack to keep it dry.

There were four dormitories inside: two for eight people and two for two, all with bunk beds. It was clean and had two good loos and a shower. We were given a room for two, in which we quickly stripped off our soaking clothes and hurried to the shower, shivering. But the Minister and his party had used all the hot water and so we towelled ourselves dry and considered what to put on. Everything was soaked except our night things and so we put on those. In my case, they were a T-shirt and Kenyan kikoi, a bright-red cotton wrap, which I always sleep in when travelling. Louella had a fairly long blue T-shirt, which just about reached her knees, and over this she put her mackintosh jacket. With thick (wet) wool socks on our feet, we looked ridiculous, which no doubt explained the cool reception we had from the Minister and his group when we made our way down to the cramped parlour, where all were gathered. There was quite a crowd on the three small sofas, one of which was entirely taken up by the Minister's extremely tall son, who did not get up to offer us space on it. The atmosphere was palpably unfriendly and when I explained to the Minister that our purpose was to encourage tourism in the lesser-known parts of Albania, he said we would do better to go along the coastal villages. He then ignored us and concentrated on flicking between channels on the fuzzy television set.

The other party had already eaten and we chewed our way through some cold, stringy chicken with cucumber and white cheese in silence. Afterwards, the Minister's 'part-time advisor', a young man called Gent Mati, who spoke good English and told us he ran a travel company, introduced me to his father, Ilir Mati, a noted Albanian journalist, who had not spoken up to this point. We established that he spoke French, not English, and after that there was no stopping us. He was full of good advice about where we should go and what we should do and I scribbled notes on the back of one of the fliers, where our route was spelled out. This he completely rearranged, giving lots of fascinating and erudite advice, only some of which was feasible in the time we had available. It was fun listening to such an enthusiast who knew his country so well and two hours flew by. During this time the Minister was becoming increasingly and visibly annoyed and he suddenly ordered everyone to bed. At which point the lights went out, as they always do in Albania in the evening, and we were left alone. With our clever head torches, we were able to stay up a bit longer to write up our diaries after a very long day. We had walked and ridden for ten and a half hours over difficult terrain, crossed a 2000 m pass and got soaked several times. We should have been unhappy but we went to our bunks giggling at the absurd atmosphere and slept, as we always do, like babies.

Mario had redeemed himself by worrying that the horses would kick each other to death if left in the little yard. He and Freddie had moved them into an orchard, where we found them tied up but happily working their way through large heaps of hay, the cost of which was included in our bill for the night. He had also been driven to a spot where there was reception for his mobile, and he had established that Mickey and Tonio had been delayed on their ferry and would not be arriving until the morning. Part of the reason for his gloom the previous evening, apart from the rain and the pain of riding such a long way, for the first time, we suspected, had been his inability to use his mobile phone. Now he was his usual cheerful self again.

When it came to saddling up our mounts, we found that the calves had sucked several inches off the leathers on Louella's saddle. Fortunately, there was just enough left to tighten the girth. With perfect timing, Mickey arrived in the Landcruiser as we were ready to set off and I was able to persuade the Minister to give an interview on camera, in which he talked about the future of Albania's tourism. He said it was having a boom year, but all he talked about was what was happening on the coast. Albania is one of a handful of countries where tourism accounts for more than a third of foreign currency earned and it will probably continue to do so for some time. The opportunities to restore the shattered economy of the remote interior, to encourage people to move back to their devastated villages and, through tourism, supplement their incomes as well as growing much-needed food, and to let the world know about this least known and most ravishing part of Europe, are legion. But we felt that they were not likely to get much help from this Minister.

That day Mickey shot a lot of good film as we rode down what is reputed to be the most magnificent gorge in the Balkans, perhaps in the whole of Europe. When I wrote to Paddy Ashdown about our journey, he wrote back that it was the one place not to be missed and it is a wondrous valley. Due to the weather, we never saw it whole, but glimpsed craggy peaks, towering rock faces and dark ravines through the swirling clouds. We were reminded of pictures of the Yangtse Gorges and of limestone cliffs in Borneo. Below the mountains which line the gorge were valleys filled with fertile soil, where handsome stone farmhouses lay surrounded by idyllic fields. All was truly rustic: the hay in cocks, the corn in stooks, the fences made of wooden palings. And through it all runs the most translucent river we had ever seen. The water in the Valbona River was a crystalline pale aquamarine, like water sometimes is in the tropics where you can see far down to the bottom. Two men were fishing for trout with a hand line and we wished there was time to stop and try out the collapsible rod and tackle I had brought from England.

I had changed horses with Mario and, by continuous repetition of 'Hetz!', I was able to urge Pieter to go faster in front and lead the others on, so that we could make better time. In the middle, the valley narrows and the cliff sides towered over us, reaching for the skies. We craned our necks upwards. The sides are still mostly clothed with trees: dense, rich beech and walnut at the bottom, sparse firs clinging to sheer slopes higher up. They must be unstable, as great boulders litter the valley floor, some of them on the road so that vehicles have to manoeuvre round them. One farm we saw had a giant white limestone rock, almost as big as the house, sitting in a field beside it. Far above, we could see the white scar on the cliff face from which it had broken loose, probably in a storm. I imagined the family cowering in their beds as they heard the fearsome rumbling getting closer.

In Dragobi, where there is a pretty village and cemetery across the river, we stopped to rest the horses and have a drink at a bar. Inside, a man was playing on a long-necked lute, a *chifteli*, while another sang in harmony. Everyone was very drunk by the time six men in leather jackets arrived in a smart black Mercedes and began to take an interest in Mickey, who was filming. Albania is reputed to have the highest Mercedes ownership in the world, almost all stolen from Germany, and I was told that the newer the car the more likely that its occupants are mafia of some sort. We thought it best to ride on. Mario was unnerved and said, 'These are not good people, like in the Shala Valley.'

After about six hours' riding, the valley opened out and we branched left up a track into Shoshan, since I wanted to avoid riding through the large town of Bajram Curri. Perhaps because Mario had decided not to trust anyone outside of his native Shala Valley, he failed miserably to find grazing for the horses from the first three farmers he asked. They either said they had no grazing or demanded a ridiculous sum. I had decided that I would pay 500 leka (about £2.50) per horse per night for grazing. Most people proved happy with this and threw in a quantity of hay or cut grass, but here the first man I asked – a shepherd with a fine moustache, who was driving his sheep into a field – refused point blank. The next group of men, who were working on the roof of a house, asked for US$150, which was of course unacceptable. After an hour, we had made no progress and I was getting fed up. Mario was for giving up and riding the horses into town, where Tonio, who had now joined us, said he had cousins with a yard. Mickey had been checked into a hotel, so that he could charge his camera batteries. We were due to join him, but I didn't want to spend two more hours riding there, and the horses needed some good grazing. Leaving the horses with Louella, I jumped into the Landcruiser and drove off down a lane which led toward the river. After another failure we struck lucky and found a truly welcoming farm, where we were greeted with open arms. There was a big field of lush grass, through which a little stream ran. Since we planned to take the next day off and visit Kosovo, the horses would have a full two days to gorge themselves and we felt they deserved it. Over bunches of grapes and sweet coffee we discussed the arrangement. The farmer, a strong, balding man called Skender Imeraj, and his wife, Spahe, said we were welcome guests and could pay whatever we liked. That approach, which was to be found more often than not throughout the country, always meant we were extra generous on departure.

Bajram Curri is not an attractive town, with a preponderance of run-down decaying tower blocks, and it did still seem to us to have an atmosphere redolent of the bad times described in such an exaggerated way by Robert Carver in his book *The Accursed Mountains*.

> The whole region was once again gripped by blood feuds and revenge killings, some over land, some over ancestral quarrels. There was no knowing how many were killed every week, but it was certainly many hundreds. Whole valleys now had no men in evidence at all: they were all hiding in the tall stone towers of refuge because of clan vendettas. In the five years since the fall of communism the region had gone right back to the state of endemic lawlessness described by Edith Durham in 1908.

At that time, in 1996, Albania was in turmoil during the collapse of the pyramid investment schemes, for which almost everyone had fallen as the country started the transition from central planning to a market economy. Albania was at that time classified by DFID, the UK Department for International Development, as the poorest nation in Europe (today it has ceded that dubious honour to Moldova). The people, who had been cut off completely from the real world by Enver Hoxha, simply had no idea how markets worked. When new banks and companies started offering to double or treble investors' money in two or three months, people sold everything they had to get a piece of the action. The mania was fuelled by money laundering from smuggling and the very first speculators were seen to be making fortunes. People sold their houses; farmers sold their livestock. At first, government ministers supported what was happening, seeing it as 'progress', even though it was manifest to all outside the country that it was too good to be true. When the schemes started to collapse, as they inevitably would, since most of them had no assets, the country degenerated into chaos. Much of the army and police force deserted and a million weapons were looted from their armouries. There are stories of MIG fighter jets being stolen from their hangars, of farmers stealing tanks. Much of the weaponry made its way to Kosovo or into the hands of well-organised criminal networks. Two thousand people were killed in six months, mostly by random shooting. In spite of great efforts to persuade everyone to part with these weapons, with offers of up to three times the black market value, most are still kept hidden by the population. Barely 10 per cent are thought to have been returned. No Albanian would sell his weapon and many families possess one or more sub-machine-guns, as well as lots of smaller guns. Arms possession is an Albanian tradition, even if now they are mostly kept hidden. We were to see and hear plenty of evidence of this. Many shepherds carried a gun and we often heard gunfire in the distance. There was widespread destruction of property: government buildings, schools, factories, mines, even orchards. An international peacekeeping force was sent in to keep control of the situation while new elections took place. It was a dangerous time, but all Albanians I've spoken to and all those who know and care for Albania told me it was never as bad as Carver described it.

We checked into the barracks of the old Intourist hotel, which we were told sometimes doubles as the town morgue, with bodies stored in the lobby. Thankfully this time a wedding was in full swing, with loud music and a bride in a tiered white gown. Both she and the groom, in white shirt and black trousers, looked intensely gloomy as they danced some distance apart, waving their arms at each other but never touching. Guests placed money on their heads or threw it over them so that it lay on the floor. Mickey had found somewhere that sold pizzas and we gorged ourselves before crashing out soon after midnight.

Chapter 4

Serbian Interlude

Kosovo lies only a short distance from Bajram Curri. It is, unsurprisingly, a strange and tortured place. Not really a country yet, but no longer fully a part of the 'former Yugoslavia', which today really means Serbia. It has had a terrible history, both in the distant and recent past, being overrun time and again by Slavs, Serbs, Bulgarians, Turks and then, again, Serbs. For a time in the Middle Ages the dominant population was Serb. It was then that most of the exquisite churches and monasteries were built and when Kosovo became the centre of the Serbian Orthodox Church, founded by St Sava in 1219, with its Patriarch based at Peç. Under the Ottoman Empire, the Albanians, most of whom had converted to Islam, prospered for some five hundred years until the empire collapsed and Serbs were in the ascendant again. Ethnic cleansing was common whenever change was in the air, and it has continued in recent years. Under Tito's communism there was relative peace and Kosovo was an autonomous province, but it was always Yugoslavia's poorest province, with the highest unemployment, combined with the highest birth rate. Slobodan Milosevic curtailed that autonomy, which led to the brutal separatist Kosovo War in the 1990s, and the violence was as bad as ever. NATO went to war with Serbia over Kosovo, and Belgrade was bombed. During the worst of the conflict, a million ethnic Albanians fled the country, only to return and displace a quarter of a million Serbs. Now the population is 92 per cent Albanian, 4 per cent other ethnic groups, and only 4 per cent Serb, who live in enclaves protected by UN troops.

I wanted to visit Kosovo, partly to see at least one of the celebrated, but now beleaguered, churches and monasteries, partly to set foot where about a quarter of all Albanians live. We took Mario only with us, as Mickey wanted to work on the film and Tonio didn't have a passport. We drove over a low pass on a road now impeccably asphalted, as this is to be one of the major routes from the Balkans to the coast. A highway is being constructed through the wild Albanian hills. When finished, it is hoped that it will do wonders for everyone's economy. We had been warned not to try to ride horses near the border. The hillsides are full of mines laid by the Serbs during the 1990s to deter both the Kosovo Liberation Army and other forces from entering Kosovo and also to injure refugees. I was even given a map of where the worst places were and on my recce I met an American who was part of a team locating and defusing mines. On the tarmac we were safe, but this was somewhere it would not be a good idea to go for a picnic, as the heaviest density of mines and other unexploded ordnance was said to be near crossing points.

We were hassled at the border, where they wanted to take our spare diesel cans off us and where I had to pay an exorbitant amount for a minimum of fifteen days' car insurance. This is a familiar feature of Balkan border crossings, as it is impossible to buy this insurance in Britain. We had had to do the same thing on entering Albania, but at least there we were using the insurance for the full period. Mario made a big scene and nearly got us arrested, but as they all seemed to be Albanians it ended amicably, in spite of his screaming 'Bullshit' at them repeatedly.

A winding road took us through rich agricultural land to Deçani, a crowded small town, where we crept through the main street in heavy traffic. There was a tense atmosphere, with groups of idle youths standing around, staring. When we tried to ask the way, people turned away, looking scared, and they denied knowledge of the monastery, which is world renowned. We came to a roadblock and I was immediately transported back to Crossmaglen, across the border from my childhood home in Ireland, where there used to be a heavily armed lookout post during The Troubles. Draped in camouflage netting, sinister gun emplacements held dark holes from which weapons protruded. Our passports were taken from us and, after a short delay, we were allowed to drive on. We were in a picturesque valley surrounded by mountains and forests, through which ran the River Bistriça. In a field on our right I spotted a heavily bearded monk in black robes herding some milch cows. It made a pretty picture. I jumped out of the car and walked up to him smiling and indicating that I would like to take a photograph. He shrank from me, shaking his head and looking afraid. I extended my hand, but he gestured wildly with his head and said, 'No photo! Go monastery!', and then I saw the dog. Behind him and being restrained by both his hands on its collar was a huge snarling mastiff, which was trying as desperately to escape and get at me as he was to restrain it. No wonder he was scared; it looked well able to tear me to shreds. I retreated hastily.

At the monastery gate, a solid low tower between high walls, there was another guard post, this time with bullet-ridden windows. We were questioned by the efficient Italian UN soldiers and let in. Immediate tranquillity. Transportation to the Middle Ages. A monk, in deep contemplation, sat against the church on a stone ledge in the sunshine. A novice in a grey tunic was cleaning out the little rivulet, which runs right round the church through freshly mown grass. Wooden-galleried refectories and cells surround the large enclosed courtyard, and rooks cawed in the surrounding trees.

The church dominates the space and is breathtaking, a Romanesque gem. Built between 1327 and 1335 by the Serbian medieval king St Stephen, it is in almost perfect condition inside and out. It is the largest and best-preserved medieval monastery in Serbia and the church is the biggest in the Balkans, with the largest collection of frescoes. Surprisingly, the architect was not Serbian Orthodox, but a Franciscan from Kotor on the Dalmatian coast, Father Vitus, and this shows in the scale and, to a Western eye, familiarity of the design. The stone is smooth and looks as though it was cut yesterday; it shines in creamy white, yellow and purple stripes of marble. Since 2004 the monastery has been listed by UNESCO as a World Heritage Site.

A tall, gentle monk called Father Hylarion showed us round the church. He spoke fluent English, as did most of the other thirty monks in the community, it seemed, as well as French and probably lots more languages. He told us that he used to be an actor and now paints icons. The whole interior of the church is covered with frescoes, more than a thousand of them, and none painted later than 1360. Many are still hardly weathered. There was a serene head of a bearded saint painted with just a few confident lines, which I stood and gazed at for a long time. Over the west door there were centaurs blowing trumpets, dragons were draped around windows and grotesque gargoyle heads abounded. Coming in from the drudgery and toil of medieval work in the fields to all this must have been more exciting than any modern television programme. The monastery at Deçani has always been a place of refuge and peace, yet now, like the twenty other Serbian monasteries in Kosovo with their two hundred or so monks, they are surrounded by hostile Albanians, who would like nothing better than to slaughter them all. Since Ottoman times all, whatever their faith, including Muslims, have been welcome to come and worship there and many still do. There are traditional holy days when the locals gather, and there have been occasions during times of serious conflict when the monasteries have sheltered as many as 150 non-Christian Albanians who were in danger. During the troubles in 2000, when Serbian troops were massacring Albanians, the charismatic young abbot, Father Sava, went out and rescued terrified families hiding in the woods and brought them to sanctuary. However, extremists see the monks as a threat and constantly harass them. In March 2007, forty mortars were fired at the monastery from the heavily wooded surrounding hills. One hit a corner of the church and knocked off some masonry.

Little has changed in the last hundred years. Edith Durham visited Deçani and described it thus:

The monastery, which lies about 1500 feet above sea-level, appeared as a white church surrounded by outbuildings at the entrance of a magnificently wooded valley, through which flows a small river, the Dechanski Bistritza, the one slope rich with stately chestnuts and the other fir-clad. Robbed of its broad lands, which have been swooped on by the Albanians, who at the time of my visit made further progress up the valley impossible, it lies precariously on the bloody edge of things, and only the wonderful white marble church tells of its former glory. It was being used as a military outpost, and twenty-five Nizams and an officer were quartered on the monastery, which had also a guard of its own, a set of Mohammedan Albanians, who were said to be very loyal. They looked like a wild-beast show, spoke nothing but Albanian, had the most elegant manners, and I was never allowed outside the monastery gate without a couple of them.

(*Through the Land of the Serb*, M.E. Durham, London, 1904.)

A passionate advocate of Albanian nationhood, she recognised the problems, calling Deçani 'an outward and visible sign [to the Serb] that this land is his'; but she firmly took the Albanian side against the Serb. Elsewhere she wrote:

The recognition of the Albanian nation and its emancipation from the toils of those who wish to absorb it is most earnestly to be desired . . . for the Albanians are the oldest inhabitants of the land – were there before the arrival of either Serb or Bulgar. The Serbs were not settled in numbers till the beginning of the seventh century A.D., and the Bulgar invasion was yet later. Bulgar and Serb each in turn built an empire and swayed the Balkan peoples, and each empire in turn fell shortly after the death of the strong man that made it . . . The empires of both in turn ruled almost all Albania for a brief period, but their frontiers were too fluctuating and their existence too short to be taken as precedents for fresh delimitation. And when both were overthrown and crippled by the Turk the day of the Albanian came . . . [The Serbians] practically evacuated their former lands, which have since been for the most part re-settled by the descendants of the original inhabitants, the Albanians. The Serbs call the territory, fondly, Old Serbia. The Albanians have as good a right to call it Old Illyria. It was Serbian once; and Calais belonged to England. The conditions of the Middle Ages no longer exist. The fierce enmity between the two races on account of this territory is a cause of weakness to both, and renders more easy the entry of a foreign invader. Could they but come to an understanding over it, they could cry 'Hands off!' to all comers, but this appears to be impossible.

It is a tragedy that, in spite of Albania becoming a nation (but without Kosovo), two World Wars and the creation of the European Union, this scrap of land is still being fought over. Since we were there the Albanian majority have declared an independence which the West recognises, but the Serbs and the Russians do not. The issue is not yet fully resolved.

Father Hylarion invited us to take coffee and we went up to the refectory on one of the great balconies. Long tables on a highly polished ancient dark wooden floor and a picture postcard view of the church. As we rose to leave, a young, but already bearded, monk arrived carrying a tray of tempting food, which he said was for us. There was freshly baked bread from their own ovens; mild white cheese, refreshingly unsalty after what we were becoming used to in Albania; a tasty spicy orange chutney and a pepper pesto; rich, sweet jam made from some local berry; and lots of green olives. Also a bottle of strong Serbian red wine, which I mixed with the slightly fizzy and saline spring water. We were offered raki, but declined. Instead, we finished with bunches of dew-fresh grapes. We were not allowed to pay, although I was permitted to leave some Euros. Leaving really did feel like crossing a boundary between two worlds and we grieved that such gentle people should be hated just because they were Serb.

A short drive brought us to Peç, the site of the patriarchal monastery and the centre of the Serbian church for centuries. More crowded streets with mainly young, handsome people, who looked at us askance and were definitely not welcoming. Once again we found it difficult to get anyone to stop and give us directions. In a bustling modern town it is hard to realise just how dangerous and precarious life has been recently for the population.

They have every reason to be scared of strangers, and yet there is a veneer of normality which insulates the traveller, at least on a brief passage such as ours. It is the fear and insecurity below the surface which can be glimpsed but which a secure traveller with a British passport is unlikely to understand.

Some of the worst ethnic cleansing of Albanians by Serb paramilitaries, police and special police, aided by the army, happened in Peç in 1999, barely eight years before we were there. The descriptions of what went on, which are spelled out in great detail in the testimony given later at the International Court at The Hague, make dreadful reading. First-hand accounts of whole families being shot in their homes by their Serb neighbours. Women being taken en masse to rape camps. The digging of mass graves. This was all as bad as any of the dreadful horrors which have been heaped on Albanians throughout their history. It is no wonder they can be suspicious, paranoid, touchy and intensely proud. It is perhaps this pride which has seen them through their terrible times and sustained them through the long periods, often of grinding poverty, in between. This was a glimpse into the eyes of the Kosovans, briefly enjoying a tenuous peace but about to face the prob-able conflict which everyone assumed would come in a month or two. The issue of independence from Serbia was due to be resolved before the end of the year. The ethnic Albanians who, once again, constituted over 90 per cent of the population, wanted full independence. Serbia, of which Kosovo was still technically a province, would settle for nothing beyond broad autonomy. The UN, who, assisted by NATO, administered the country, advocated 'supervised independence'. There was no common ground and the Albanian-dominated provisional government had announced that they would declare independence on 10 December. America backed the Albanians; Russia the Serbs. More conflict loomed and inter-ethnic violence lay just below the surface. It had flared up only three years before when some Albanian children were drowned in a river and extremists went on a rampage.

We were in a conflict zone, but it didn't feel like it as we drove out on an excellent asphalt road to the turning for the monastery. Here, at the entrance to the Rugovo Gorge, there was another formidable guard post draped in camouflage. This time our passports were taken from us and Mario was told that he must stay in the car while we made our visit. We passed nuns working in the fields, as twenty-six of them now look after the monastery and the church, with occasional visits from priests and, presumably, the Patriarch himself, as this is the mother church of the Serbian Patriarchate.

A young Italian NATO soldier with a long multicoloured bobble on his cap escorted us through the gate into the monastery. There we were greeted by a sweet, elderly nun in an elegant straw hat with a purple and yellow bandana, who took us under her wing. Wisps of grey hair escaped to frame her smiling face. Unlocking the church, she showed us round, explaining everything in good English, but in a frail, exhausted voice. The church is more than a hundred years older than Deçani, having been built in the twelfth century, and the earliest paintings are from 1250. Inside, it is darker and the paintings are harder to see. Sharp faces surrounded by golden haloes sprang out at us from the gloom. Occasional shafts of sunlight revealed how much colour, hidden for centuries, bright lights would unlock. The church was plundered by the Turks for the first time at the end of the seventeenth century and it took nine horses to carry away the treasure. Now, some restoration is being done and there is a great feeling of tranquillity and spirituality, but underlying this is the insecurity and fear which, for different reasons, we had felt in the town. The nuns' residence is away from the church and sometimes they are stoned by Albanians as they run the gauntlet.

Waking Mario, who was asleep in the rear seat of the Landcruiser, we drove back over the hills into Albania proper. On the way, we diverted to visit Tropoja, birthplace of Dr Sali Berisha, the Prime Minister of Albania. It is described in the usually reliable *Blue Guide*, last published in 1997, when Berisha was President, as 'a charming, unspoilt rural centre, with very attractive Ottoman-period buildings around a small square'. It is no longer like that. Now most of the buildings are in ruins and it is not in the least picturesque. We felt that something terrible must have happened there and, not wanting to stay and find out what it was, we left without stopping. As we drove away, we had a good view over the village of the craggy peaks of Mount Shkelzen shimmering in the pearly evening light. They are the final thrust of the Dinaric Alps, which run all the way south from Italy. They are the most rugged and extensive mountains in Europe after the Alps and the Caucasus, containing the most sizeable areas of limestone and having given the name *karst* to science. It is their impregnable slopes and gorges which have kept this corner of the world so isolated for so long.

Bajram Curri, that frontier town, supposedly full of gunslingers and blood-feuds, felt quite like home. We found Mickey in the internet café, where he had been uploading clips of film of our ride onto our website. Already diaspora Albanians from as far away as Chicago were emailing the site to say how glad and grateful they were to us for trying to put Albania on the map.

Chapter 5

Blood-feuds

'The most important fact in North Albania is blood-vengeance, which is indeed the old, old idea of purification by blood. It is spread throughout the land. All else is subservient to it.'
Edith Durham, *High Albania*

The horses had had a good rest and were looking distinctly fatter after grazing lush pasture for thirty-six hours. Skender and his family of wife, three sons, a daughter and two nephews, who all lived in their tiny, clean, swept cottage, welcomed us openly, so that we were made to feel at home. They had a wonderfully archaic tractor, a healthy-looking crop of maize, various fruits and peppers drying in the sun, a cold-water standpipe in the yard and a magnificent view back up the Valbona Gorge. They seemed content with their lot and delighted with my proffered payment for the grazing. Repaying hospitality and spontaneous generosity is always difficult, especially in a country where both are regarded as obligatory and money, apart from payment for grass and hay, would be an insult. And so we always carry presents. On this ride, Louella had decided to bring some cheap but pretty pashminas to give to our hostesses, woollen gloves for children and some excellent wind-up torches, which of course required no batteries, for men. These were a brilliant choice and always went down well.

We were heaped with good advice about the way ahead, which took us round the back of Bajram Curri and well away from built-up areas. It looked easy and we began to make over-optimistic plans about where we might reach by nightfall. Distances are deceptive on maps, even detailed ones like ours, and the locals, we were to find, were wildly optimistic about how much ground our horses could cover in each hour. On that day I could see that a quite high pass lay ahead, but what I had failed to spot was that two deep ravines would have to be crossed first. Our kind hosts told us it would take us an hour to reach the top. It took us five. At first, there were wide views across open plains, with low, rounded mountains behind, markedly different from the savage peaks surrounding the Valbona Gorge. But through these plains ran rivers and they had carved channels several hundred feet deep, which were invisible until we arrived at the edge. Then we would have to dismount and lead our horses down steep and stony goat paths, across a rocky river bed and, if we were lucky, up a cattle track on the far side. Once, there was a rather shaky suspension bridge. To my surprise, Louella's Billy stepped bravely across when she led him onto it and Mario followed with John. I had changed horses with Mario, as I found that Pieter, in spite of his twisted foot and smaller size, was faster and allowed me to lead, which I preferred. I was the map reader and the only one with a clue about where we were going, even though I was all too often wrong about how to get there. Pieter absolutely refused to cross the bridge and so, ignominiously, I had to lead him down another steep bank and across the almost dry river bed.

It was blisteringly hot that day, which always makes distances expand. Time dragged as we headed south-east towards the cleft in the mountain range ahead which marked the pass. At a village called Luzhë, we glimpsed movement in a garden and called out, but no one came. The place appeared deserted, but we needed directions. A warm wind blew through the mostly ruined houses, but the people, if there were any, kept out of sight. Frustrated, we rode on and, round a corner, came on a nice-looking boy of about sixteen in shorts and a striped T-shirt. He was happy to give us directions and, indeed, to walk part of the way with us so that we should not get lost. But first he insisted on inviting us into his house for some water. This turned into an instant meal of a chunk of good fresh bread, a tomato, a gherkin and a lump of salty white cheese each. It was just what we needed to speed us on our way. His name was Liridon Beçi. He and his younger brother walked with us for half an hour to put us on the right track and told us it would only take twenty minutes to the top. Faint hope. It took us that long to reach a place where there were springs and a pretty green dell. Here there was good grass and deep mud caused by some cattle, watched over by an old man further up the hill. It was a perfect spot for a house, with a glorious view back the way we had come, but it was also impossible to find a way through for the horses. Mario called to the old man for directions, which sent us floundering into some thick scrub intersected by impassable gullies running with water. It was some time before we had found a way through the thorny undergrowth and could begin the steep climb to the top, following a narrow path. By now we were exhausted and Louella was suffering, as she had caught a filthy cold, probably as a result of being soaked to the skin three days before. We made it and were rewarded with views in all directions, including down to the village of Vlad on the far side, which I had intended to be our rendezvous and, perhaps, where we might stay the night. Tonio was supposed to have found us a field there and somewhere to stay.

I had chosen Vlad because I hoped it might have some link with Dracula: Vlad the Impaler. Legend has it that both Vlad, a Romanian prince, and Skanderbeg, born George Kastrioti, who were contemporaries, were taken as boys to be companions for the son of the Ottoman Sultan Murad II. At his court they were taught philosophy, Greek, Hebrew and Latin as well as how to fight; and they probably learned about the cruel tortures, such as impaling, for which Vlad was to become infamous. Kastrioti became a great fighter for the Turks and was rewarded with the title Iskander Bey, meaning Prince Alexander, after Alexander the Great. This was transliterated to Skanderbeg. Soon after, he switched sides and fought for Albania against the Ottoman Empire for twenty-five years until his death in 1468.

Albanians have always been heroic fighters. After the country eventually fell to the Ottomans in 1479, ten years after Skanderbeg's death, many warriors sought asylum with the Venetians, who called them *stradioti*. In time they became pioneers of light cavalry tactics, which were to be much in demand throughout Europe. Carrying a spear, a mace and a dagger, they used hit-and-run attacks, ambushes and feigned retreats, which were dramatically successful. Contemporary descriptions have them remaining incessantly on their horses, 'moving like birds' and taking no prisoners, but cutting off the heads of their enemies. Their favourite weapon was a short lance with iron points at each end known as an *assagaye*. They used these to bring down the horses of mounted knights, who could then be easily killed. Wilfred Thesiger once showed me an *assegai* he had been given by Chief Buthelezi of the Zulus. He told me that this short stabbing spear had been the secret weapon which had brought Shaka, the great Zulu king, success in over-powering much of southern Africa in the early nineteenth century, killing more than two million members of other tribes. Somehow both the design and the name, *assegai*, made their way from Africa — for it is an African word — to Europe and back over the centuries, bringing conquest in their wake.

During the sixteenth century, *stradioti* were to be found fighting for the French under Louis XII, for the Spanish and the Hapsburgs under Charles V. There were Albanian mercenaries in Henry VIII's armies in England and France and gradually they were to bring about the replacement of the old, heavy, and in its day impregnable, cavalry with the new light cavalry, from which many modern regiments, including Merlin's Light Dragoons, are descended.

Today, thirty Albanians are fighting beside NATO troops in Afghanistan. Merlin, having graduated from Sandhurst and joined his regiment, was posted there during the time we eventually spent riding through Albania. It was partly to take our minds off worrying about him that we decided to travel then.

We never did reach Vlad; instead we found to our surprise that there was a new road running over the pass, which we could have followed and which would have made our lives much easier. But it was not marked on my map

and no one had thought to suggest it. This is Albania. We were now able
to contact Mickey and Tonio on our Walkie Talkies and we learned that they
were waiting for us in a bar at a place called Paç (pronounced Patch) some
way further on. Predictably, Tonio had done nothing about finding anywhere
for us or the horses to stay. The prime purpose of having a backup vehicle
was to avoid tired riders having to organise everything themselves at the
end of a long day, but somehow this message never quite got through during
our time in Albania. It took us another couple of hours to reach Paç, an
unprepossessing cluster of houses at the top of another pass, through which
a cold wind gusted. We found a depressed Mickey, who had been unable to
film all day, sitting in a noisy bar surrounded by drunk and fairly unfriendly
unemployed men. Evening was drawing on, but no one seemed to have any
idea what we should do. The horses were extremely tired and, after their
promising start in the morning, had reverted to a reluctant snail's pace,
needing constant urging to move at all. Louella was sick and it seemed
sensible to stop, but Paç was not the place to stay. Leaving our horses tied
up outside the bar, Mario and I drove on to the next village, a much more
appealing collection of farmhouses called Çorraj. Here, at the very first
farm where we stopped and asked, a sensible, calm young man agreed that
we could stable our horses. He had to consult his widowed mother first. I
left Mario to discuss the possibility of us being allowed to sleep in the farmhouse too, and drove back to Paç. Sending Mickey and Tonio back to the
farm, Louella and I slogged on for another hour, mostly downhill and
leading Mario's horse, to arrive just as darkness was falling.

Amazingly, we found that all was perfect harmony. Although the farmhouse was quite small and already occupied by two families, the mother and
three sons downstairs and a family of cousins upstairs, we were all made
welcome. The horses were put in a yard and given armfuls of fresh hay from
one of three hay cocks, each of which was crowned with a waterproof cape
made of plastic sheeting to stop the rain getting down the central pole. Next
door was a tiny barn with calves and chickens. Everything was neat and tidy.
The house was equally well organised. Cooking was done under the entrance

porch, where there was also a sink and all the cooking utensils were hung up. On the ground floor, there was a front room, which was given over to us, although everyone kept coming in and out to watch what we were doing. There were two lumpy sofas for Louella and me to sleep on, an alcove with a curtain for Mickey to make his nest in. Mario and Tonio were taken upstairs. The bathroom was a pleasant surprise. Spotlessly clean, there was a basin loosely attached to the wall, a squat loo, and above it a shower head, which actually produced some hot water. We had not been expecting such luxuries.

Having washed, we all sat in the parlour and talked, secretly wondering if there was any chance we would be fed. Once again, Albanian hospitality came up trumps. From nowhere and with no warning, our hostess produced mounds of excellent pasta – far more than we could eat – accompanied by tomato, cucumber, bread and cheese. This we washed down with thick, creamy milk with a crust on top – something I hadn't seen since I was a child – several glasses of fiery raki and finally little cups of thick, sweet Turkish coffee.

Sabrie, the mother, was dressed in black. She had a kind, oval face and looked much too young to be a widow. We asked what had happened and she told us readily, through Mario. Six years before, her husband, then aged forty-five, had been shot and killed in a dispute over water. Within half an hour, her eldest son, Shkelqim, then aged seventeen, had taken his father's gun and shot the murderer. Because he was so young and patently justified under customary law, he had only served a year in jail. Later, he was to join us, black bearded and gentle; he didn't look like a killer. Much behaviour, especially in the north, used to be governed by the Kanun of Lek Dukagjini, a code of honour dating back to the Middle Ages that orders property division, marriage rituals and many other customs, most notoriously blood-feuds, where retaliatory killing is justified for the maintenance of family honour. The countryside, especially in the Shala and Valbona valleys, used to be filled with kulas, semi-fortified, defensive towers built of stone with little holes to serve as windows. In these, men would live for years in order to escape a revenge killing. As soon as a man was killed, one of his relatives would be honour-bound to kill the assassin; and so it went on indefinitely. The huge patriarchal clans ignored, over the centuries, laws imposed by first the Ottomans and then by King Zog. Only under communism did they begin to give up the old ways, but they are far from forgotten. Ismail Kadare, Albania's greatest writer and inaugural winner of the International Man Booker Prize in 2005 for his brilliant novel, *Broken April*, tells the story of a young man who is forced to commit a murder under the laws of the Kanun. As a result, his own death is sealed and he waits to be killed by a member of the opposing family. Kadare characterises the north of his country as 'a universe of legends, the land of fairies and oreads, rhapsodists, the last Homeric hymns in the world, and the Kanun, terrible but so majestic.' Blood-feuds do still occur, although they were strictly forbidden under communism and great efforts have been made recently to stamp them out. However, in this case, because the issues were so clear cut, Shkelqim's action had ended any potential feud and they told us there was no problem in their relationship with the murderer's family. There used to be twenty families in Çorraj; now there are only six. Everyone has left, said Shkelqim.

Another tradition which is dying out is the practice of creating 'sworn virgins'. For various reasons, including if all the men in a family were killed in a blood-feud, or if a girl decided she did not want to marry the man chosen for her, a woman might become the head of the house and take on the role of a man. When she makes this change she swears to remain a virgin for the rest of her life, but she can achieve far greater status than she would ever have as a woman in the still extremely patriarchal world of the rural north. She takes on all the attributes of a man, such as smoking, drinking alcohol and even carrying guns and knives. It is an honourable thing to do, when there is a need, and is in many ways preferable to the downtrodden role women still fill. In Edith Durham's day things were even worse for women. In *High Albania* she describes a long debate she had on the subject:

Blood feuds, they said, were almost all the fault of women. Women were wicked . . . Sometimes they were very disobedient, and you had to beat them a great deal. A man must order his wife three times before he may beat her, and then if, for example, she still refuses to go and fetch water, what can he do but beat her? I suggested that, perhaps she was tired and the water-barrel was heavy. 'Oh no,' was the reply, 'they are quite used to it.' Also, if a man tells his wife not to answer him, and she does, he must beat her, or she would go on talking. Of course, only a woman's father or husband may beat her.

Wife-beating, said I, is punished in England by imprisonment – the King disapproved of it also. This staggered everyone – even the Padre.

Those were brutal times and Edith Durham also described how head-hunting was still being practised when she was there. During the nineteenth century it had been common, with literally thousands of heads being removed from the dead and dying during battles, to be carried triumphantly tied to the victors' belts or mounted on stakes. I have often defended head-hunting tribes around the world, who have been perceived as profoundly primitive, by pointing out that this was a practice still widespread in Europe within living memory.

Great interest was taken in our preparations for bed and we wondered if everyone was going to sleep in the room with us, since there was precious little space elsewhere in the house. But the lights went off at 10 pm, as usual, and as soon as we started to take our clothes off, they said goodnight and left us. In the night there was a noisy thunderstorm followed by heavy rain, and at 6 am, when the single bulb in our room came on and we woke up to the sound of cowbells and cocks crowing, it was still raining. We didn't want to test their hospitality further than necessary and so packed up quickly and saw to the horses. I went out early to the yard to see how they were and found them looking miserable and wet, standing with their heads hanging down. We had always intended to sell them at the end of this first week of travel. Looking at them, I began to think the sooner the better. Sabrie came out of the cow byre carrying a pail of steaming hot milk from their cow and gave me a big smile. By 8 am we had saddled up, it had stopped raining and we were ready to leave. We paid the family generously for all we had received (it was for the horses and their feed, of course) and gave them presents. Sabrie was overwhelmed and smothered Louella with kisses. We waved energetically as we set off up the steep hill behind their farm.

Our first destination was a place called Kam, the site of one of the most important acts of sabotage that SOE carried out in Albania during the Second World War. At that time it was a major chrome mine, with a German garrison of 120 and some 400 'slave labourers': Albanians and other prisoners of war being forced to work the mine. On the evening of 30 January 1944, three British soldiers slipped past the guard patrols and crawled towards the mine's machine shed, which controlled the tackle used to transport the ore through the mountains. In charge was an RAF officer, Squadron Leader Andy Hands, aged thirty-two and described as 'a short, active and aggressive little fellow'. With him were two NCOs, Colour Sergeant W. Brandrick and Corporal Ivor Clifton. They killed both the sentries silently with a knife and laid plastic explosive all over the machinery. There was a massive explosion and the mine was never worked again. Hands received the DSO and Military Medals went to Brandrick and Clifton.

The vehicular road to Kam wound around the mountain, making a big loop. After Kam we were put on a path which would take us over the top and so save us a lot of riding. From Kam it should only take three or four more hours along dirt roads to reach our final destination for this part of our journey at Helshan. Beyond lay Lake Fierza, the largest of three great lakes created under Hoxha's communist regime to generate most of Albania's electricity. On my recce in July, I had tracked down a man who said he could ferry our horses across to Kolsh, the village where I had arranged to collect our next pair of better, lowland horses. It would be a very long way to ride round via Kukës and anyway I had resolved not to ride through a town on this journey if I could help it. When I went to inspect the boat, it had proved to be rather small and made of rusting metal. It was powered by a 5 horsepower motor and, at about 5 metres long, looked incapable of carrying three horses, even small ones. But the ferryman assured me he often transported animals in it and there was nothing to worry about. Moreover, if we could get to Helshan, which was up a long finger of the lake, created by a flooded valley, he said it would only take about three hours to travel all the way to Kolsh on the other side, far quicker than riding for another day to the spot opposite. We negotiated, and he agreed to take one of the horses as payment. In Kolsh, I had met a nice man, who had indicated that he just might be interested in buying the other two.

Louella, when I showed her a picture of the ferry, was extremely dubious and said it looked sure to sink. She had been worrying about this plan of mine for some time and my airy reassurances were beginning to wear thin, especially as our horses liked nothing better than to try to kick each other whenever tied up within reach.

As we reached the top of the ridge, after an hour or so of riding to begin with and then leading the horses up the final steep incline, it began to rain again in earnest. I had quite a good waterproof coat, which I attached to my saddle in a stuff bag, but I had not thought to bring the accompanying overtrousers. Louella's coat let the water through and Mario had lost his little umbrella. The far side of the ridge was covered in thick scrub and we were soon lost. As we neared the abandoned farms outside the village, things got worse, as the paths were overgrown with brambles, which tore at our clothes, and the gateways had been blocked with branches, which we had to pull apart. Miserable, cold and soaked through, we struggled into Kam at last, and a more ill-favoured place would be hard to imagine. A cluster of ruined buildings, only one of which showed any sign of life: a tenement block with washing hanging out of a top-floor window. The rest of the place was derelict, but we dragged our horses out of the rain into the first large structure, which we were told later had once been a hospital. The floor was covered in sheep dung, with nastier human excrement in the corners, and the wind howled through the missing windows. We unsaddled the horses and took them out again to stand despondently tied up in the rain. We hastily stripped off – easier said than done – as the wind and the rain drove through the windows, unpacked some dry clothes from the Landcruiser, which arrived at that moment, and flapped our arms to try to keep warm as we struggled into them. Two small boys appeared and they were put to work looking for firewood. In the end, the best supply was obtained by wrenching out the remaining couple of window frames. In no time we had a roaring fire going. Although it smoked dreadfully and made everyone's hair and faces black, it cheered us all up.

Now was a time for some serious planning. We had ridden our mountain horses to the lake, which we had been able to see from the top of the hill before the rain arrived; Louella's cold had become much worse and I worried about her catching pneumonia. Trying to ferry the horses down the lake would be even more risky in a high wind and it suddenly occurred to me that we really didn't have to do that anyway. If I could sell them now, all our current problems would be resolved and we could go and stay in a hotel in Kukës. Mario said that one of the drunken men in the bar at Paç had said he wanted to buy the horses. I thought this seemed most unlikely, but it was worth a try, so he and I drove back there, taking about half an hour. Meanwhile, the others huddled over the fire, becoming blacker by the minute. Hoping to ignite a spark of greed for a bargain, I told Mario to offer all three horses for the knockdown price of £120 for the lot and to explain that this was only because we were desperate.

I sat in the vehicle, while he went into the bar to negotiate. Incredibly it worked, and after fifteen minutes he came out with the money. Taking into account the fact that I didn't now have to give the ferryman one of the horses, I had effectively sold them for about half what I had paid. Or to look at it another way (and at that moment I was ready to look at it any way that justified going to a hotel, rather than try to camp at Kam), I had paid less than £10 per day per horse; a lot in Albania, but well worth it for us to have been able to make the ride. It was also what I had agreed to pay to borrow the next two horses, on which we would be continuing the journey. In a glow of contentment and self-congratulation, Mario and I hurried back to tell the others. Even the four-hour journey to Kukës, for much of which we were able to average no more than 7 miles an hour because of the appalling condition of the road, failed to dampen our spirits.

To celebrate, we stayed in the best hotel, the Amerika, the top floor of which had just been refurbished. The intermediate floors, all eight of them, had not been done up yet, nor had the lifts, and so we lugged our bags up past gaping holes, into which it would have been all too easy to stumble and plummet back to earth. Our rooms were spacious and it was a merciful relief to be able to collapse onto a large bed. The décor and fittings were the very latest in both fashion and technology, if a little overambitious. In particular, a decision had been taken to have everything operate by sensor rather than switch. Only the installer had failed to set the timings correctly. This meant that although the lights came on when one went into the bathroom, they went off again as soon as one sat on the loo or stayed still for a moment. We had to keep our arms waving about at all times to see. There were no handles on the taps. Instead, water was meant to come when hands were held near them. And sometimes it did, although the wash basin was very reluctant to deliver. The bidet, on the other hand, squirted water across the room whenever one walked past it. But these were small prices to pay for being under cover and warm.

In the hotel Amerika there was great enthusiasm for shooting, with lots of stuffed pheasants and partridges, as well as heads of wild boar and deer, on the walls. The owner pressed me to stay for a few days and enjoy some sport, but I had to decline. A distinguished Cornishman, Sir Arthur Pendarves Vivian, Member of Parliament for Camborne, used to take his gamekeeper and spaniels to Albania and shoot the marshes around Butrint. His 1876 diaries, which I tracked down in the Cornwall Records Office, having been tipped off that he had travelled in Albania, turned out to be mostly game books recording bags of between twenty and forty woodcock each day, supplemented by quantities of snipe and an occasional wild boar. A letter from the British Consul at Patras in Greece, who seems to have arranged these trips for Sir Arthur, includes this encomium: ' . . . you have done wonders and your good shooting will never be forgotten by the peasants at Kanali, who gave you the name "Devastation".'

He was not alone in going to Albania for the shooting. Maximilian, Emperor of Mexico, travelled down the coast in 1867, shortly before being arrested and executed by the republicans back in the country he had only ruled for three years. He went shooting on the coast near Durres.

One family which lived in Corfu during the 1930s was the Durrells, who were made famous by two of the sons, Lawrence and Gerald, both to become successful authors. In his delightful book, *My Family and Other Animals*, Gerald describes an expedition across the narrow strait to Albania by the middle brother, Leslie, then aged nineteen.

This was the shooting season: on the mainland the great lake of Butrinto had a fringe of tinkling ice round its rim, and its surface was patterned with flocks of wild duck. On the brown hills, damp and crumbling with rain, the hares, roe deer, and wild boar gathered in the thickets to stamp and gnaw at the frozen ground, unearthing the bulbs and roots beneath. On the island the swamps and pools had their wisps of snipe, probing the mushy earth with their long rubbery beaks, humming like arrows as they flipped up from under your feet. In the olivegroves, among the myrtles, the woodcock lurked, fat and ungainly, leaping away when disturbed with a tremendous purring of wings, looking like bundles of wind-blown autumn leaves.

Leslie, of course, was in his element at this time. With a band of fellow enthusiasts he made trips over to the mainland once a fortnight, returning with the great bristly carcase of wild boar, cloaks of bloodstained hares, and huge baskets brimming over with the iridescent carcases of ducks. Dirty, unshaven, smelling strongly of gun-oil and blood, Leslie would give us the details of the hunt, his eyes gleaming as he strode about the room demonstrating where and how he had stood, where and how the boar had broken cover, the crash of the gun rolling and bouncing among the bare mountains, the thud of the bullet, and the skidding somersault that the boar took into the heather. He described it so vividly that we felt we had been present at the hunt. Now he was the boar, testing the wind; shifting uneasily in the cane thicket, glaring under its bristling eyebrows, listening to the sound of the beaters and dogs; now he was one of the beaters, moving cautiously through waist-high undergrowth, looking from side to side, making the curious bubbling cry to drive the game from cover; now, as the boar broke cover and started down the hill, snorting, he flung the imaginary gun to his shoulder and fired, the gun kicked realistically, and in the corner of the room the boar somersaulted and rolled to his death.

There are great opportunities for Albania to develop field sports for tourists as, for example, Hungary has done so successfully. Much of the interior of the country is wilderness and elsewhere we saw little sign of game shooting, although we were constantly flushing partridges as we rode along. We did often hear shooting, and most Albanians do have guns, but whether they were shooting for the pot or at each other we never found out.

PART II

Guerilla Country

Chapter 6

New Horses, New Crew

We were now entering the Central Highlands, a remote, inaccessible region where, traditionally, patriarchal, feudal communities lived in isolated valleys. Many of the British SOE operatives, who were parachuted in to join the guerillas during the Second World War, were dropped among these hills, where they were well able to dodge German patrols. The people were mostly staunchly anti-communist, and many remained so for some time after the war ended. There were still almost no roads and I had met no one who had travelled there.

Our new horses were due to arrive the next morning. However, in true Albanian fashion, a series of garbled mobile phone calls relayed breakdowns and delays so that they did not make it until after nightfall. I had chosen Kolsh as the rendezvous because on my recce Mario and I had driven across the preposterously labyrinthine road through the bleak central Albanian mountains and this was the first point from which it looked possible to ride south. Mario and I had made friends with the head man, a calm, wise, elderly figure called Hassan Dheshi, who quickly grasped the idea of what I was planning and was full of good advice. He it was who had directed us to the now unexploited ferryman, but he had also said that we were welcome to base ourselves in his village, and to stay in his house if we wished. He knew the roads and horse tracks to the south and even expressed an interest in buying our first three horses when we had finished with them. We had taken to each other and I was looking forward to meeting him again.

As we drove the short distance out from Kukës, we could see across the artificial lake the mountains we had just crossed. They were covered with snow down to about a third of their height and we thanked our lucky stars we had no more 2000 metre passes to cross. We had made it just in time, as the rain we had suffered from had been falling as snow a little higher up.

Kolsh was as I remembered it: a run-down little place, some distance off the main road and full of cheerful children. Hassan greeted us warmly and was unfazed by the demands we warned him we were about to make of his household. These began when a very small trailer arrived, into which were squeezed our two new steeds. I had met Arjan Rugji, their owner, on my recce, at Pezë, about 11 miles outside Tirana, where he kept some thirty horses. I rode some of them in a grassy glade where there is a huge war memorial to those who were massacred on that spot by the Italians in June 1943. Although so close to the capital, Pezë was from the start of the war the main guerilla base from which Italian convoys were attacked and many of their soldiers killed. At last, in retaliation, 14,000 troops from six black-shirt battalions and some carabinieri were sent in against the 500 or so partisans. More than 300 houses in the village were burned and fifty-three men, women and children were killed. Their graves lie in simple rows and it is tragic to see the names of so many young boys who died fighting.

Arjan, who is President of the Albanian Horse Racing Federation, told me that he was trying to re-create the Albanian horse, which had almost vanished by the end of the communist era when riding was considered a bourgeois activity and horses were destroyed for the perceived sins of their owners. Now only the remnants of the breed were to be found still being used on farms and by gypsies. Known for their 'freedom of movement, agility in difficult terrain, disease resistance and endurance', the lowland breed, *Myzeqea*, sounded just the job for us.

Prince Leka, whom I also saw several times on my recce, told me a story about his grandfather, King Zog's, horse. He had a black Arab stallion called Hannibal, who twice saved his life. Once, in 1918, when he was leading his troops in battle, they came to a bridge. Hannibal resolutely refused to cross, which was completely out of character. The whole column was halted and had to wait while the cause was investigated. Explosives were found under the bridge, ready to be detonated. Another time, when travelling through the lagoons near Shkoder in the north of the country, Hannibal stopped dead and would go no further. Scouts were sent ahead and thirty Serbians were discovered, waiting in ambush.

Surrounded by a noisy small crowd and in pitch darkness, illuminated only by our head torches, our two horses were unloaded from the little trailer. Not surprisingly, they were quite nervous. First out was Chris, Louella's mare, which I had ridden at Pezë and liked. She looked fit and well, better than I remembered. But then anything would have looked better than the three we had just sold.

At Pezë I had selected for myself another mare, a good-looking black called Tina. I had ridden her bareback and she had seemed very strong. Unfortunately, Arjan had called me to say that she had gone lame and it would not be possible to cure her in time. He had therefore sent me her five-year-old son, Semi. He, like Chris, was a grey and, as I led him out of the trailer, I was surprised by how tall he was: the best part of 16 hands, we guessed. He was also skinny, so that his ribs showed and he had several small cuts on his legs and one on his head from where he had knocked himself on the journey. He didn't look fully grown and I began to worry that he would not be up to the journey ahead. I had quite a job persuading him to go down a slope into the shelter that had been prepared for them, where a large pile of hay waited, and he snorted with fear. I blew into his nostrils and calmed him down. He had a soft nose and was to prove to have the gentlest character and the stoutest heart of all our Albanian horses.

The next day we tried out the horses in a field near Hassan's house. This time it was my turn to be nervous, as I mounted something which felt twice as high as what I had become used to over the previous week. Semi was skittish and reared up on his hind legs, which was not a good start. Louella and Chris were getting on better and I followed behind them as we made a gentle circuit of the field, walking, trotting and even breaking into a controlled canter. It was not a moment to fall off, as half the village was watching. So, too, were our new 'crew'. These had been found for us by Auron Tare, who had helped me hugely on the recce and who hoped to join us towards the end. Auron, the leading Albanian expert on Butrint, the wonderful archeological site in the far south, which he had been instrumental in revealing to the world, had a house down there, where I had stayed in June. There I had met Ylli (pronounced Ulli, and named after the Illyrian god-king), who had organised several camping trips for Auron. He had agreed to be our 'camp master'. This meant that he would be in charge of putting up our tents each evening, cooking supper and generally taking that huge responsibility off our shoulders. He spoke not a word of English, but had a charming manner, was always smiling and exuded an aura of competence. He was also a blacksmith, I was told, which could come in very useful.

Our new driver, Durim, had taken some persuading to come. His normal job was to drive tourists in his taxi in and out of Butrint and this earned him good money, which I was forced to match, as we badly needed a driver for the Landcruiser. His other role was to be our interpreter, since from now on we would be on our own and unlikely to meet anyone who spoke English. Louella immediately identified him as a clone of the film star George Clooney. He didn't speak much and we were to discover that his entire vocabulary in English appeared to consist of 'No problem'. To this was soon added 'Landcruiser' and his eyes gleamed as he saw the monster vehicle he would be driving. It was to become his pride and joy, which I was seldom allowed to drive from then on.

Durim, Ylli and the driver of the horse trailer, who left early, had all stayed with Hassan. He had taken them and us under his wing and, with typical Albanian hospitality, fed everyone and allowed us to invade his space without demur. Now we began to sort out our stores, which it was just possible to load onto the Landcruiser and its roof rack, but only just. Before we left home, Louella had devised a system of packing everything into four large, strong plastic boxes with lids and it was important that everyone knew exactly where everything was supposed to be. Nothing is more frustrating than looking for a vital spanner at a moment of crisis and finding that it has made its way into the cooking box. They also meant that we could unpack rapidly on arriving somewhere we were going to camp and, even more importantly, repack efficiently in the morning. With baggage, tents and sleeping gear for five people, two large containers for spare parts and spare saddles and other horse kit, as well as a couple of sacks brought by Durim and Ylli, which we assumed contained cooking stuff, the roof rack was going to be severely overloaded. We had already found that the nuts holding it on shook loose on the very bumpy roads and we had nearly lost it on the pass into the Shala Valley. In Kukës I had found a helpful garage, where, in addition to servicing the Landcruiser, they had made in a day some stronger clips with which to hold the roof rack in place; but even with them it was going to be touch and go. I looked into buying a small trailer to carry our heavy gear instead. As things turned out, that would not have been a good idea. The tracks ahead would have demolished it on the first day.

We also needed to dry and clean the tack we had brought with us from Cornwall and used on the ride so far. Saddles and bridles were laid out and well polished with saddle soap. Then we fitted everything to our new horses. We made sure the girths wouldn't rub by always encasing them in sheepskin sleeves, and we spent a lot of time finding the best of our three saddles for the two very differently shaped horses we were now to ride. Durim and Ylli helped us. We saw at once that Ylli was good with the horses and this was a big relief, as we would be able to leave them safely in his hands; Durim made it plain he did not have much time for them, which was hardly surprising in a taxi driver. Sadly, he also proved to have little interest in anything else we were to see on our travels, which, combined with his lack of English, was to create many frustrating moments. However, his commitment to the Landcruiser was total and that was of equal importance.

For a while, all went well. We trotted along the perfect surface of the dirt road and our vehicle went ahead to give Mickey time to film us approaching and passing. The scenery was outstanding, with snowy mountains in the background and Arcadian farmsteads and neat rectangular crops in the valleys below. I had photocopied in colour all the maps, so that I could give our driver an identical map to the one I was navigating by. In theory that would mean that we would always be able to find each other. But it didn't work out that way. We arranged to meet them where the clearly marked side road to Surroj peeled off. There we planned to enjoy the packed lunches with which the hotel in Kukës had provided us and which, to save them from being jiggled about and pulped on the horses, we had put in the Landcruiser. We reached the junction but there was no one there. They had either driven past or, knowing that we would be taking it, decided to go down the side track and continue until it ran out and became suitable only for horses. There was no signal on the mobile. It turned out that they had driven past, and so we missed out on lunch.

Nonetheless, the countryside we now rode into lifted our spirits. We followed a good cart track between fields of maize and grass, where contented cows grazed. There were little vineyards and decorative stooks of hay around the homesteads. Friendly children stared in amazement and waved as we rode past their houses and old men assured us that this was the way to Arren. We felt that this was how long-distance riding should be. After a while we entered woodland and the track became a logging trail, rutted where tree trunks had been dragged. A stream ran through a deep valley and tracks branched off in all directions. It was hard to see from the map which side of the valley we should be on. We followed some promising leads, which led to dead ends, so that we had to retrace our steps, never a popular move on horses. But we were still in high spirits and when we finally burst out of the top of the wood and over a ridge we were rewarded with an open meadow carpeted with autumn crocuses. Also known as meadow saffron and naked lady, because the flowers have no leaves round them, they are deadly poisonous and there is no antidote. I had never seen them in flower like this before, but they were very common in Albania in September. They were to be a gorgeous accompaniment for the rest of our journey south, providing a flash of brilliant pink in all sorts of unexpected places, like deep woodland and barren rocky hillsides.

We could now look down a wide valley and in the far distance a winding road, which we knew from the map, climbed steeply up from the valley floor to Arren. We were high up and would have to drop a long way down before climbing all the way up again. Half way along the valley, the map showed the track dividing into several dotted lines, one of which headed south-east, straight for Arren. We found the point where a well-used path left the meadowland and disappeared into the scrubby wood which covered the hillside. By my compass, it was going the right way and could be none other than the one we sought. Dismounting, we led our horses for half an hour steeply uphill until we reached the ridge. 'We should hit the road in about five minutes,' I declared confidently. We didn't. Instead, the track, from which there had been no opportunity to deviate, started to veer off to the east and then to the north. It was very frustrating, as I knew that Arren lay no more than 3 kilometres at the most on our left. But thick forest and steep ground lay between us. We couldn't face going all the way back down to the bottom of the valley again, and the path was now heading away from Arren, so we decided to cut across country on a compass bearing. A bad decision. The wood was full of tracks, which petered out and disappeared. Sheer slopes confronted us and when we tried to skirt them we found ourselves pushing through dense undergrowth and encountering jumbles of jagged rocks. It was limestone country and we were in an area of dolines, or sinkholes, which are about the worst places to take a horse. They must have wondered what had happened to them and it was surprising neither of them was hurt. At one point we were able to lead them to the top of a hillock and from there we had a clear view of the village houses, which seemed no distance away. But as soon as we dropped back into the wood it was impossible to go in a straight line and we were floundering again, scraping the saddles against tree trunks and scratching ourselves on thorns. We were beginning to wonder if we would have to spend the night out, and our nerves and good humour were wearing thin, when we hit a proper path and, soon after, the road we had been seeking for two hours. We could now see the houses of Arren ahead, but it was a spread-out village and it still took some time before we could track down our team.

They had stopped on a pleasant patch of bare grass outside the school, where a standpipe gushed water constantly, creating a green area of marsh. It was a good place to camp, but although they had been there for some time waiting for us they had done nothing about setting up camp. We were knackered and would have enjoyed nothing more than to ease our weary bones in one of our comfortable camp chairs with a cup of hot tea. Instead, we had to galvanise our team into action, showing them how to set up our first proper camp. I scrambled up onto the roof rack, undid the straps holding our big trunks on, and began to hand down what was needed. It was important to demonstrate the priorities, in the hope that our team would get the message and do it themselves in the future. First job: see to the horses. I had bought a sack of Sweet Meadow Herbal Mix from my feed merchant in Cornwall and we now broached it for the horses. They thought it delicious and I was relieved, as they had had a hard first day. Iron stakes were hammered into the ground, long ropes attached to the horses' head collars and they were left to eat and graze.

The priorities of the horses dealt with, we turned our attention to making camp. We had brought a special tent for Mickey; one which folded flat like a giant plate, but sprang into shape when released. The locals, who were beginning to gather, were suitably impressed. Mickey was given his sleeping mat and bag and set about making his home. Our tent was another clever arrangement lent to us by my son, Rupert. It was designed to be attached to the back of the Landcruiser and so give lots of space. With the rear seats down, there was plenty of room for us to sleep in the back, once the stores had been removed; or we could lie on the ground and use the tailgate as a writing table. We had folding seats for all and a couple of collapsible metal tables, which went under a lightweight canopy tied to the side of the vehicle. Ylli and Durim had brought their own tent, which proved to be no more than a liner and was missing poles.

Now it was time to start cooking supper and we looked expectantly at Ylli, whose talents in this field had been highly praised by Auron, and who was supposed to have brought all that was necessary in the way of cooking pots, would be over in five. By now we were becoming suspicious of such travel estimates, but we had no idea how wildly wrong he would turn out to be.

At first, all went well and we rode out of camp along a good track. We waved cheerfully as Mickey filmed us heading due south. Ahead, through a dip in a low ridge, we could see the Ndërshenë Pass, which lay about half way to the park boundary. Through our binoculars, it looked an easy climb, with farms visible almost to the top of the valley. Our track cut through the ridge and turned sharp right. There was no warning, but my stomach lurched as I saw that straight ahead the land dropped away sheer for 1500 feet. It felt like being on the edge of the Grand Canyon and vertigo made me shake so that I could barely look at the magnificent view or photograph it. Semi seemed to take a delight in walking on the very edge of the void along which the track now led and I trembled as pebbles he kicked up tumbled into echoing space. Louella, who is much braver than I am about heights, was unfazed but she agreed the view was special. Like a Leonardo painting, all was in harmony; a succession of clumps of trees and clusters of houses dotted the space below and rose to the far horizon. At such moments, the aches and pains and frustrations of riding across unfamiliar, unmapped country fell away and for a happy moment we gazed in awe.

This was the first of an infinite variety of views with which our senses were to be deluged over the coming weeks. Not wild and savage as in the Accursed Mountains to the north, but Arcadian. Even if the farms were perched on the edges of yawning chasms, they looked tranquil and rustic, surrounded by neat fields. Little were we to guess then that most were abandoned and, defying all my rules of travel, few had unobstructed paths between them. It has been one of the guiding principles of my explorations that if there are two places marked on a map there is sure to be a well-used route between them. This principle has served me well in places as remote and different as the Amazon rainforest and the Sahara desert, but it simply did not seem to pertain in Albania.

As I recovered my composure, I pointed out the attractive village of Gur Reç on the far side. With a cluster of houses around a little mosque with a white minaret, it looked close enough to reach out and touch, but it was to prove elusive. Below us, on a fertile shelf, lay some houses and fields, the village of Arrëz, looking like children's toys they were so small and far below. With a sinking feeling, we realised we would have to descend to the very bottom of the gorge before climbing up the far side.

We made our way down to the farms below, passing few people on the way. These we hailed with an airy *'Mirë dita'* (Good day) and, pointing ahead, added 'Gur Reç?' 'Gur Reç!' they answered happily, and we assumed that meant we were on the right track. We were wrong. The map showed a 'trail' down to the river below Gur Reç where it met a 'track', indicated by a bolder line. When we reached the farms of Arrëz, which all appeared to be abandoned, with not a soul to be seen or heard, the land dropped away, again sheer, but now covered in scrub. We started to search for the trail without success. At last, in desperation, we led the horses along an old, dry leat or watercourse which we felt must eventually cross any path leading downhill. It was overgrown and changed from a stone channel to a rotting wooden one, where it had been built out over steep scree. We had some scary moments but at last reached an empty house where we stopped to rest. It was a delightful place that, had it been located in the Dordogne or Tuscany, would have been worth a fortune. The main doorways of the houses in this region were grand, with stylishly rounded arches. An external stone staircase led up to a balcony below a shingle roof and all around it grew the most delicious vines of black grapes on which we and the horses gorged ourselves. But still no path down to the river, although I made a wide search on foot along the cliff edge, and we had to scramble back uphill before we found it: a steep and stony goat track. At the bottom was a lopsided suspension bridge, barely wide enough for a horse. To my surprise, Semi allowed me to lead him across and Louella and Chris followed. According to my map, we should now be joining the more substantial track running beside the river towards Gur Reç. There was a faint path leading upstream and along this we led the horses. I soon realised that something was wrong. This was no proper track leading to a village; it was merely the way sheep and goats reached the pocket handkerchiefs of pasture beside the river. When it began to peter out, I sat down and examined the map again. I had mistaken the dotted line indicating a track for the only slightly larger one indicating an administrative boundary. The River Mollës was the boundary between the districts of Kukës and Dibër. There was no track.

And so we had to retrace our steps to the bridge, where we found a better path leading downstream, away from where we wanted to go. This brought us to a substantial farmhouse, where there was a good spring of water for the horses to drink from. While they were doing this, two teenage boys came and greeted us. Once again we asked the way to Gur Reç. This time there was no doubt. A rough, steep trail led up the hill behind the farm and back the way we did want to go. Without waiting for further hospitality which would be sure to be forthcoming if we hung around in such a remote place, we said goodbye and hurried on. The day was beginning to slip away from us and we could not afford to linger. After a while, the elder of the boys caught us up and made it clear he had come to show us the way. He was not going to allow us to get lost again. Half an hour later, as we struggled up and up, his younger brother arrived carrying a bag with warm bread and thick chunks of the white, salty cheese we had become so accustomed to. It was a genuine gesture of true hospitality to strangers and we showed our appreciation by doing our best to eat as much as possible. Not easy, as both bread and cheese were hard and dry. Good, honest boys, they saw us to the point above Gur Reç where our route headed up towards the pass; and they genuinely tried to refuse the 500 leka notes I pressed on them. By now, we had taken six hours to do a journey we had been told by the schoolmaster in Arren would take us two; and we were not yet half way to Lura.

A long climb to the top of the pass brought us to more dramatic views, now of increasingly forested country, and then once more downhill. We met some shepherd boys, who were no help with directions, and we struggled on, finding successive new ridges to cross and becoming increasingly exhausted. At long last we reached a proper road, which even showed signs of having been driven on at some point, and we followed this hopefully down a wide valley. Evening was drawing on and with it came flocks of sheep and goats and herds of cattle, all heading home to their villages and harried by barking dogs. We joined them and found ourselves dropping down into the wide, grassy valley where Fushë Lurë lay, the village where we had arranged to meet our crew. 'Fushë' means 'meadow' in Albanian and it is a common prefix to place names, sometimes denoting that it is a village near a larger place. Of course, there was no sign of Durim and Ylli, but people we accosted seemed to know something and we hurried our very tired horses in the direction indicated. This was not the way to the spot I had marked on Durim's map, but I was beginning to learn that maps did not mean much to him. As darkness fell and the rain began to fall, we spent a deeply frustrating two hours searching for our vehicle. *'Po! Po!* [No! No!] *Landcruiser!'* one boy exclaimed, and pointed back the way we had come. Another insisted we should go to the 'Tourist Hotel', of whose existence we were not aware. We suspected we were just being sent there because we were those rare creatures, tourists. But eventually, after much to-ing and fro-ing, we were persuaded and set off up a steep and very bad road into the woods and the dark. For twenty minutes we struggled on, then decided that this was madness as there seemed to be nothing ahead. We were now far from the village and the road was so bad we felt sure the Landcruiser could barely have made it. And so we retraced our steps to the bottom of the valley, where we were greeted by more interested locals. All this time, I had been trying to call our team on my mobile, but failing to get a signal. When they saw this, they now led us to a certain tree some way from anywhere and here they assured me I would get a signal. At that moment the phone rang. It was Auron, calling from Tirana to ask us where we were! He didn't know where the Landcruiser was, but he knew the crew were looking for us, as they had called him. Then Durim got through and said 'centre of village', before he was cut off. We wondered what to do. One of the local men asked me if I wanted to sell the horses. I said I'd think about it. At that moment, we saw headlights coming down the road we had ridden up. There was, indeed, a tourist hotel up there and, as they had not made camp in the village as instructed, that was where we were going to stay. We staggered up the hill again to find a large unfinished building in the middle of a recently burnt wood. We unsaddled the horses to find that Chris was developing a saddle sore. We fed the horses and tethered them where there was a

Chapter 8

Through Lura National Park

It was surprisingly chilly high in the mountains; something I had not taken fully into account, as it had been scorching hot during my recce in June. We only had a sweater and a fleece each and often slept in them, as well as starting the day wearing them before the sun raised the temperature. We were in the saddle by 9 am and set off south along the road marked as running the length of the Lura National Park, followed by the Landcruiser. It was possibly the worst driving road I have ever been on. This was because the only other users were occasional, vastly overloaded, logging trucks which ground along at less than walking pace and made ever deeper ruts. In wet places and where it had rained it looked more like a trucking road through the Amazonian rainforest than a European road. This was fine for us on horses, but on the verge of impossible for our 4x4. Fortunately, it was probably the best vehicle made for the job and Durim, for all his other faults, was a superb driver. Having to crawl along, often slower than we could walk and trot, he nursed the Landcruiser tenderly over rocks which lay ready to rip out the sump, teetering on one side with one wheel between the ruts and one half way up the bank. The only damage done during a long day driving the whole length of the Park was to the plate to which the tow hitch was attached, and this was constantly battered and bent.

Information on the Lura National Park had been scanty. In the tourism literature put out by the government, it is described as occupying an area of

1,280 hectares, lying at an altitude of about 1,350 to 1,720 metres above sea level and having 'great possibilities for developing eco-tourism'. The glacial complex of the Lura lakes is styled 'one of the most beautiful pearls of Albanian nature'. But no one seemed to have been there and, apart from the tiny hotel, there appeared to be no infrastructure. Instead, the Park is being systematically robbed of its lovely rare trees, such as the Heldreich, black, white and red bark pines and ancient beech trees, by illegal loggers, who act with impunity in this remote area. Large tracts of forest had recently been burned and we rode through acres of blackened trunks and scorched, bare ground where the ghostly silhouettes of twisted branches and the absence of all small animals and birds, except for a few jays and crows, created an eerie silence. This was broken only by the sound of chainsaws far away and high up. Melodious warbling from above intrigued us, until we discovered it was a muleteer driving four mules and a horse, each carrying substantial planks of freshly sawn wood. Smoke from recently lit fires drifted up from the hills all around, perhaps started by goatherds hoping to encourage the growth of vegetation from the ashes. A healthy forest does not make for good pasture.

The scenery we rode through was as grand as it gets. Deep gorges, their sides clothed with pines clinging to the bare rock, framed plummeting vistas which made me dizzy. The craggy mountains above are said to harbour wolves, brown bear, lynx, wild goat, stone marten and deer, as well as wood grouse, partridge and capercailzie, but we saw no sign of these. Nor did we see anywhere in the country the swarms of tortoises, 'oddly fascinating beasts that bask in the sun and peer at you with little beady eyes', which Edith Durham describes in *High Albania*.

There are fourteen glacial lakes of breathtaking beauty in the Lura National Park. We only saw half a dozen of them from the road and the first two were virtually empty dams. We stopped to picnic at one of them, unsaddling the horses and letting them graze on the rushes and sweet grass by the water's edge. There, our team, who had been having a difficult time negotiating the dreadful road surface, caught us up and we all shared our sandwiches and apples with the animals which, having had no hay the night before, were ravenous. The prettiest lake we saw was the relatively small four hectare Flower Lake, *Liqeni i Luleve*, which was surrounded by water lilies. If there had been fish it would have been an idyllic spot, but I saw none rise on any of the lakes and in many places the scenery was marred by yet more fire-blackened hills.

The going was good for our horses that afternoon, with open valleys where we could even let them canter briefly, although they were tired after the long previous day. In this way, we went faster than our backup vehicle, which was able to do little more than a walking pace. A logging truck overtook us, grinding methodically along the ruts, which the smaller Landcruiser had to try to straddle. We followed the truck across a wide marshy area, where each preceding vehicle had made its own track. Beyond, the road made a wide loop to the bottom of a valley and we took a short cut through the woods down a steep slope to rejoin it. Soon after, we stopped to wait for our team to catch up. They took a long time to do so and we watched a shepherd driving his flock towards us, accompanied as ever by large barking dogs. We gave him one of our fliers and tried to explain that we wanted to reach Selishtë by nightfall, riding over the pass ahead, while our vehicle went round by road. By signs and emphatic pointing, he made it beyond doubt that we were going the wrong way and had missed the turning, which lay further back. I was pretty sure from the map that both routes should have gone through the gorge we could see ahead and if the others had caught up with us I would have tried it; but they must either have broken down or gone another way and so there was nothing for it but to retrace our steps. As it was already 5 pm, this was no time to be separated and so it was with much frustration that we trudged back up the hill. Near the place where we had last seen them, we found a much-used track leading off to the west. This was not the way the logging truck we had followed had gone, which was how we had missed it. Now we were in the unfortunate position of being behind our support vehicle with them thinking we were ahead and doubtless hurrying to catch us up. All we could do was follow as fast as we could urge the horses; of course, there was no signal on the mobiles.

After a while the road improved and it became apparent that we had missed the short cut over the pass and were taking the long way round. We came over a ridge to see that the land dropped away into a deep valley ahead, while the road looped and snaked its way along the right-hand side. I thought I glimpsed the flash of a rear light as something vanished round the very last corner. Assuming it was the Landcruiser, we hastened on. Two hours later we reached the corner. Several deep gullies had lain in the way, each requiring a drop to its floor and back up again. Once again, darkness was falling and we had been riding for ten hours. To our left, the last of the sunshine caught a limestone pinnacle of exquisite beauty, which guarded the end of the valley above a narrow chasm. Perched incongruously on its edge like a Dalek was one of Hoxha's pillboxes. Ahead we saw that the road wound steeply to the river far below and there, to our relief, we saw the vehicle climbing back up to meet us.

We camped by the river after dark. There was a strong flow of icy water to wash in and some good grazing on the bank for the horses. The only small area of fairly flat ground was right next to the road and that was where we camped. Mickey had a bad neck from the bumpy drive and chose from then on not to sleep in his tent. Instead he reclined in the front seat of the Landcruiser, which he said was more comfortable. Strangely, he never snored there, which was just as well, since we were sleeping at the other end of the car and would have had to throw things at him if he had. His tent was given to Ylli and Durim, whose useless piece of thin canvas didn't keep the cold out, let alone the rain. The gas stove had been broken on the drive and so Ylli cooked delicious soup and pork chops over an open fire of branches that we had gathered from surrounding bushes.

During the night our camp was raked from time to time by the headlights of lorries, since this was now a road more travelled than the one through the Park. At 5 am one stopped and there was a loud altercation as Ylli and Durim told them to go away, while they insisted on hanging around and checking us out. As they left, Durim muttered, '*Mafia!*' Soon after, a mule-teer rode past with tinkling bells and our horses decided to follow him. They were attached to iron pegs, which were quite easy to pull out, and so by 6 am we were all up and warming ourselves round the embers of last night's fire. As the sun rose, three tiny children aged about three, four and six drove some cows past us on their way to pasture. The smallest two were holding hands and each clutching a crust of bread, their only food for a day as they watched over their parents' cows. From our horses we were able to pluck red and yellow plums from the hedgerows, as well as big fat blackberries, which we munched happily along the way.

In the substantial village of Selishtë, which we had hoped to reach the night before, the young men gathered to offer advice on our route. This, as usual, was conflicting and Durim was of little help; he merely shrugged his shoulders and walked away muttering, 'Bad people, stupid people.' This was an improvement on his usual vocabulary, but failed to help us obtain the detailed directions we needed if we were not to spend another day lost. Finally, an old man joined the cluster of people and when I showed him my map and indicated Fushë Bulqizë, he nodded vigorously and with a gnarled finger traced the route we should take. He even offered to help us on our way. The others would be driving round the long way, leaving us to cross a series of passes. The old man assured us that it would take no more than three hours riding and, as we were heading due south and on the map it was only 12 kilometres as the crow flies, we were naïve enough to believe him. He waved us off at the point where a promising trail began, a kilometre south of Selishtë. We made good progress through apparently prosperous farming country, where the small fields grew tall crops of corn and where we could look down into farmyards where horses and mules were being loaded up for the day's work. We reached the top of the first pass in good spirits and feeling very fit. I knew it was hubris to think it, but I couldn't help being pleased with how surprisingly well I felt. Despite the excessive amounts of exercise we were taking, nothing hurt. I did a mental check: feet OK, in an ordinary cheap pair of trainers and thick wool socks, no blisters; back feeling strong, with only occasional aches and twinges; no headaches; tummy OK; and not out of breath or at all tired as we strode up to the top, just stopping every hour or so for a few minutes' rest. I felt a flush of euphoria as I realised how lucky I was that I could enjoy the moment and the view to the full, without the distraction of pain. Looking back the way we had come, we could see a vista of medieval splendour. Wild mountains, their sides painted with brush strokes of greenery, swept down to gentle combes where the homesteads looked halcyon, each one a perfect abode. Distance blurred the reality of the harshness and poverty of the lives lived there and the gentle autumn colours softened what was soon to become bleak and snowswept. We trudged on, Louella dragging her reluctant horse up what we thought was the final steep incline of the pass. Her cold was better, but she was still not feeling fully fit and found herself short of breath. I encouraged her by saying that now we were at the top it should be all downhill for the rest of the day. Not so.

For the next five hours we walked, leading the horses along obscure paths which, for the first two hours, continued to rise inexorably. Instead of dropping down to the floor of the next valley, as I had hoped, we found ourselves forced ever higher through mature forests of beech and oak. The going was punishing as we scrambled around obstructions, negotiated gullies and slithered down screes. In the early afternoon, deep in woodland, we came to the highest point and there we unsaddled and let our mounts graze. They were always hungry and quite indiscriminate in what they ate: beech leaves, reeds, thistles, fir trees, ferns. We gave up trying to persuade them that some of these were bad for them and they seemed to suffer no ill effects. It began to rain heavily and so we saddled up again and put on our wet weather gear. This made us sweat, but we had to keep our cameras and notebooks dry. From now on we had mud to contend with, as the soil became sticky and black, dangerous for horse and man alike, especially going downhill. When at last we emerged from the trees onto an open ridge, we could see the Landcruiser far, far below on the valley floor and the red splash of Mickey's tent. For once, they were making camp in anticipation of our arrival, although it was another two hours before we were able to reach them.

On the way, soon after we had been able to remount again, we stopped at the first house outside Fushë Bulqizë, a modern construction with a prosperous-looking family who came out as we rode past and insisted we stop for a large glasses of thick foaming buttermilk with them. I found it welcome and delicious, but Louella had a problem choking it down. They insisted we had seconds, by which time she was looking decidedly sick. We tore ourselves away and with their good directions we were soon riding into our camp, which had been set up in a field next to a copse of willows, the whole scene framed by a rainbow gleaming through the steady rain.

I had some serious planning to do. Somehow, we had to get to the main road that runs across the middle of Albania at a place called Librazhd, where I had established on my recce that it would be possible to cross and continue south. Some roads had been marked on some of the maps I had acquired, but we were learning that this did not mean they were passable, even by our 4×4. We were advised that the best way to drive from Fushë Bulqizë to Librazhd and Elbasan, where we planned to stop for a couple of days in a hotel while the horses had a rest, would be to go a very long way round via Albania's capital, Tirana. We should be able to find a more direct way across country, but there was no question that on our very tired horses we would make it in less than two days. Without a guide, it would be very difficult both to find the way and to arrange for somewhere to stay each night, since our backup could not reach us and we would be on our own. Mickey had made friends with the head man of Fushë Bulqizë, who had allowed him to put his batteries on charge in his office, which was quite close to our camp site. We went to see him and explained the problem as best we could, using Durim as our interpreter. Several locals had piled into the office to take part in the discussions and everyone was trying hard to be helpful. A young man was produced who claimed he could get us and the horses to Librazhd in eight hours. This seemed too good to be true and I said I would pay him 10,000 leka, some £50, if he would guide us. We even shook hands on the deal. Then it transpired that he was talking about driving there and that he knew nothing of cross-country routes for horses. A lot of time had been wasted and Durim, who must have known it was all nonsense, just shrugged and left the room. It looked like we would be on our own.

Chapter 9

Hard Times in the Hills

It was about now that a guardian angel came into our lives and started working miracles. We do Bed & Breakfast on our farm in Cornwall and a year or so before this, when I was just beginning to think about riding through Albania, a couple picked up on our plans. 'We have friends who live in Albania,' they said. 'They are missionaries and their home is in Elbasan.' I had exchanged emails with Nick and Sar Wakeley and we had made plans to meet. I now telephoned Nick on my Albanian mobile and explained our predicament. He immediately took over our lives. First, he explained clearly and simply in perfect Albanian to Durim exactly what it was we planned to do and what we expected of him. Then he gave directions for driving round to Elbasan and said he would meet him there. He would book Mickey into a good hotel, where he could work on the film, charge batteries and access the internet. Meanwhile, Louella and I would have a lifeline whenever there was a mobile connection, as he could translate our needs to any Albanian we met as we made our way through the interior. Suddenly things began to look up, although we still had plenty of worries. Not least among them was the condition of our horses, who were becoming tired and had not enjoyed their night out in the pouring rain, in spite of the armfuls of hay we had secured for them from a local farmer. Moreover, Chris's saddle sore was getting worse.

We awoke to what Edward Lear calls 'a very mistiferous morning' with 'the cold-Cumberland feeling of these mountains after rain'. At 6 am we climbed back into our wet clothes, but I could hear a nightingale singing in the copse behind us and the promise of reaching Elbasan for some rest cheered us up. It was a couple of hours before the sun broke through and then everything started to dry quite quickly. By 10.30 we were on our way again, heading from Fushë Bulqizë to the larger town of Bulqizë, where we had to shop for some essentials, such as cards to top up our mobiles, as it looked as though we would be using them a lot over the next few days. It took us about an hour and as the sun rose in the sky it became hot. This road was asphalted and, as Albanians seem to feel obliged to do, the drivers went as fast as possible, hooting as they passed us, which made the horses shy. I waved each car down as they approached, but it made no difference. Someone threw a plastic bag out of a minibus, which nearly hit my horse's head. It was full of sick. We cut across the valley, avoiding the traffic and the main town, to a satellite conglomeration of horrible communist-era tower blocks, which lay more directly on our route. Dust and litter swirled about us as we rode into one of the most depressing places I have ever seen. All the buildings were crumbling and looked ready to fall down. Some of them had gaping holes through which rubble and concrete flights of steps could be seen. Paper bags and indescribable rubbish lay everywhere on the ground among the wrecks of cars and rusting pieces of metal. Yet there were strings of washing hanging outside several windows, children played among the debris and dogs skulked. Here we met up with our team and a crowd gathered. No one had much idea what lay up in the hills beyond the town.

We loaded ourselves up with small but quite heavy rucksacks containing some basic essentials as we did not know how long it would be before we would see our team again. As the midday heat intensified, we began to climb up a winding road to the south. It was very hard work and slow going, and with our increasingly reluctant horses refusing to move at more than a crawl, it was faster to walk and drag them. For five hours we ground uphill, once again taking far longer than the relatively short distance on the map had led me to hope. This was because the road zigzagged to a ludicrous degree.

Every time we thought we were approaching a point where we would cross a ridge and thus be able to see ahead, there would be another one. When at last we had a view, we found that another great chasm lay between us and our objective, with still more twisting tracks to endure before we got there. There were few opportunities for short cuts, which in any case often proved more arduous than sticking to the road and going the long way round. It began to dawn on me that we were not going to make it to Librazhd, which lay barely 25 km due south, in the two days I had estimated. We were more likely to take a week at this rate – assuming the horses would be able to go on that long. Louella's horse's saddle sore was not going to get any better, even though we were now walking most of the time. I began to think of alternatives and decided to call on Nick Wakeley's help.

Fortunately, there was a signal for my mobile and so I was able to talk to him. I explained our predicament and asked him if he knew anyone with a truck who could pick us up the other side of the mountain and drive us and the horses to Elbasan. He immediately said he did. He also knew a vet who would inspect the horses to see if they were fit to continue and he even knew someone who would stable them for us. Nick checked with the truck owner to find out where in our direction the nearest road-head was and called back after an hour or so to suggest a place called Bizë, which was marked on my map about half way between Bulqizë and Elbasan. I had been told by the head man in Fushë Bulqizë that it was possible to ride to Bizë, but no one had a clue how to cross the country beyond and the map was of little help. We agreed that Nick and the truck and our crew, to whom he would explain everything, would meet us the next day at Bizë. We would sleep somewhere on the way. It was a huge relief to have resolved what was becoming an impossible dilemma, but we still had quite a long way to go.

One of the pleasures of long-distance riding is that it gives time to talk together without the distractions of daily life. And then there are long periods of silence, time to think about what we are doing and why: the history of the country we are riding through and the experiences of those who had roamed there before.

A hundred years before our ride, Aubrey Herbert travelled adventurously in the Balkans, where he acquired a wild Albanian highlander as bodyguard and servant. Kiazim, who could not return to his country because of a blood-feud, became passionately attached to Herbert. Wearing his national dress of a spotless white fustanella or kilt, topped by a scarlet sash into which were stuck a jewelled pistol and dagger, he would beat and sometimes almost kill anyone who jostled his master in the street. He was taken back to England to his master's estate, Pixton, in Somerset, where he caused a sensation among the staff. There was a pheasant shoot soon after he arrived and Herbert, who had failed to explain things to Kiazim, sent him to escort a late-arriving gun to his stand. The first drive began while they were still on their way and people began to shoot at the birds. Kiazim, suspecting an ambush, threw the startled guest to the ground and lay protectively on top of him, with a drawn revolver in one hand and a dagger in his teeth. Next day, Herbert kept Kiazim with him, but was disconcerted to see him decapitating the fallen pheasants with his dagger.

John Buchan, in his classic spy story, modelled Greenmantle (Sandy Arbuthnot) on Aubrey Herbert. It is a tale of courage and disguise about a Holy War in the Islamic Near East, and although written in 1916 it resonates today with peculiar echoes. Greenmantle's adventures seem unbelievable and yet while reading about Albanian history I have come on stories by British undercover agents which equal any of Buchan's fiction. I love the part in the book where Sandy is introduced for the first time. It fired my own early enthusiasm for adventurous travel when I first read it as a child:

Lean brown men from the ends of the earth may be seen on the London pavements now and then in creased clothes, walking with the light outland step, slinking into clubs as if they could not remember whether or not they belonged to them. From them you may get news of Sandy. Better still, you will hear of him at little forgotten fishing ports where the Albanian mountains dip to the Adriatic. If you struck a Mecca pilgrimage the odds are you would meet a dozen of Sandy's friends in it. In shepherds' huts in the Caucasus you will find bits of his cast-off clothing, for he has a knack of shedding garments as he goes. In the caravanserais of Bokhara and Samarkand he is known, and there are shikaris in the Pamirs who still speak of him round their fires. If you were going to visit Petrograd or Rome or Cairo it would be no use asking him for introductions; if he gave them, they would lead you into strange haunts. But if Fate compelled you to go to Lhasa or Yarkand or Seistan he could map out your road for you and pass the word to potent friends. We call ourselves insular, but the truth is that we are the only race on earth that can produce men capable of getting inside the skin of remote peoples. Perhaps the Scots are better than the English, but we're all a thousand per cent better than anybody else. Sandy was the wandering Scot carried to the pitch of genius. In old days he would have led a crusade or discovered a new road to the Indies. Today he merely roamed as the spirit moved him.

The story of Greenmantle was based on the idea, fostered more famously by T.E. Lawrence, that an Englishman could become an Arab and understand Arabs' problems better than they could themselves. The female anti-heroine in the book *Hilda von Einem* was modelled on an Englishwoman who filled that bill as well as either Herbert or Lawrence. Gertrude Bell, the intrepid Arabian traveller and writer, who was to be largely responsible for the creation of the state of Mesopotamia, later to become Iraq, was a brilliant academic, being the first woman to gain a first-class degree in History at Oxford, as well as the greatest woman mountaineer of her age, an archeologist and a linguist. She was also rich, unhappy and prone to falling passionately in love.

During my research for this book, I kept coming across the names of three Englishmen with double-barrelled names, and I kept confusing them. They were Lt Col. Charles Doughty-Wylie VC, Capt. Duncan Heaton-Armstrong and Col. Dayrell Oakley-Hill. Sorting them out has given me another view of my country's continuing involvement with Albania, in addition to the literary, political and active military/guerilla activities. This was service by British officers on secondment, many of whom came to be fascinated by Albania and some to love it.

Doughty-Wylie has a double connection with this story. He was an extraordinarily brave soldier who had fought in India, the Sudan, where he took part in the capture of Khartoum, in the Boer War and in China. He it was with whom Gertrude Bell fell most deeply and hopelessly in love when she was in Baghdad and he was military consul and head of the Red Cross in Turkey. He had a wife, Lilian, but it was not until he was posted elsewhere that Gertrude could bring herself to set off on what was to become her most important expedition: to the oasis of Ha'il. The place to which he was posted was Albania, where he was to be Chairman of the Commission appointed in 1913 to delimit the Greek and Albanian frontier. This was a tricky assignment and there are many on both sides today who would still question the validity of where the border was drawn. I was unable to track down any notes of his from this time, but his wife's diaries are in the Imperial War Museum and they reveal how frustrating it was to try to separate Turkish and Greek villages. She complains constantly about the recalcitrant behaviour of the Frenchman on the commission, who always took a contrary view. They did a lot of shooting for the pot, as food was hard to get, chamois and partridge being plentiful. She describes long journeys by horse, often in search of eggs, and she was frequently stiff at the end of the day.

At the outbreak of the First World War, Doughty-Wylie was sent to Gallipoli and took part in the first landings, when there was terrible loss of life. Among the papers in the War Museum I found his last letter home. It was to his mother-in-law in Wales telling her what to do if he was killed, which seemed likely. She was to go straight to France, where her daughter, his wife, was working in a hospital on the front line at St Valéry-sur-Somme. She would need her mother to look after her, he wrote. The next day, 26 April, carrying only a walking stick, as he refused to shoot Turks, with whom he had spent so much time and whose language he spoke fluently, he led the charge which took a formidable Turkish redoubt. Both he and Capt. Walford, who was by his side, were killed at the moment of victory and both received the VC. Doughty-Wylie was buried where he fell and his is today the only individual Commonwealth war grave on the Gallipoli Peninsula.

On 17 November 1915, a small boat brought ashore the only woman on the Allied side to be given special permission to visit Gallipoli during the campaign. She walked up to Charles Doughty-Wylie's grave, where she laid a wreath. It was his wife Lilian. There is, however, a persistent rumour that she was not the only visitor to his grave that month. Gertrude Bell had met him in London earlier in the year and they had exchanged love letters which are full of guilt as well as premonition of his death. She never married and was to die ten years later from an overdose of sleeping pills. Lilian lived on until 1960.

Duncan Heaton-Armstrong, an adventurous Irishman of independent means, accepted the post of Private Secretary to Prince William of Wied. He, too, was a brave man, unlike his master, and he did his best to make the unlikely crowning work. He had no time to learn any Albanian, but he was quite impressed by the people who came to greet the king.

> Some of the hardy mountaineers that came to pay homage were about as fine-looking specimens of semi-barbaric manhood as one could wish to see, and decked out in their best clothes made a very fine picture. Though unfortunately many of these patriots were not in the habit of squandering their fortunes on soap, and had strengthened themselves for this auspicious occasion with a mouthful of garlic, their manners were naturally graceful and their bows often as elegant as those of any courtier in Europe. Some of them were splendidly arrayed, their short jackets one mass of gold lace and embroidery. Around their necks they wore massive silver chains of quaint workmanship, to which in ordinary life revolvers were attached . . .

During the troubled months he spent in the country, he bluffed his way out of danger several times by claiming to be British. He found this 'seemed to please them', and wrote,

> The British were very popular in Albania as the people still remember the time when we occupied the Ionian Islands, which were later handed over to

Greece. The Corfiotes were very satisfied under British rule and it is said were exceedingly sorry when the British left the island; from there this sympathy spread to the mainland.

Edith Durham, however, did not have a high opinion of Heaton-Armstrong. She told Aubrey Herbert that he was 'the wrongest man for his post that could have been found. His nickname of the chocolate soldier exactly hits him off. He tells everyone that he only came for the pay.'

After the assassination on 28 June 1914 of Archduke Franz Ferdinand, heir to the Austro-Hungarian throne, by Gavrilo Princip, a Bosnian Serb member of the Black Hand, a pan-Slavic secret society, a chain reaction of war declarations broke out. By August, it was obvious that a British officer could not remain in the service of a German, however loyal he was. Albania was starting to break up and it was decided to send the king's children to Munich with the two German ladies-in-waiting. Heaton-Armstrong volunteered to escort them across Italy and Austria to Germany, and he was given safe-conducts for all three countries. On arrival, the Germans broke their pledge and he became the first prisoner of war. He was exchanged after two years and eventually reached the front in January 1917. He survived and lived in Herefordshire until his death in 1969.

Dayrell Oakley-Hill was recruited in 1929 into the gendarmerie set up by King Zog and commanded by General Sir Jocelyn Percy. This was to bring relative peace and stability to Albania for the first time and it was a remarkable achievement while it lasted, establishing smartness and efficiency of a level not seen in the region before. Under Zog there was also exceptional religious tolerance, especially for Jews. Later, during the Second World War, as many as 3,000 Jewish people were given shelter and none was handed over to the Nazis. When the Germans took over the occupation of Albania from the Italians in 1943, the population refused to comply with orders to provide lists of Jews residing in the country. This assistance, in a predominantly Muslim country (incidentally, the only one in Europe), was based on *besa*, the code of honour which makes hospitality sacrosanct. Alone in continental Europe, there were more Jews in Albania at the end of the war than when it started.

Oakley-Hill, described as 'a short, wiry, vital man', and his wife Rosamond were posted to Elbasan and immediately fell in love with the country. Sometimes accompanied by Rosamond, Oakley-Hill made a series of very long journeys by horse all over the country and covered many of the routes we were to follow later, including the Valbona and Shala valleys. He rode a 'nice-looking grey pony, about 14 hands, who was . . . sure-footed on the mountain tracks'. A keen naturalist and photographer, his book *An Englishman in Albania* captures the feel of the country well. He learned to speak Albanian and remained an ardent supporter of all things Albanian for the rest of his life.

During the war, he joined Julian Amery, whom we are about to meet, to fight with the resistance movement in the northern hills, before being taken as a prisoner of war when Belgrade fell to the Germans. Released due to ill health in 1943, he went back to Albania with UNRRA (the United Nations Relief and Rehabilitation Administration) to try to help the new communist administration. Disgusted with Hoxha's attitude to aid, he eventually resigned. He describes Hoxha as having 'a diseased imagination born of paranoia'. Hoxha, by contrast, describes him as 'a mad enemy of the Albanian people'! Later, he was to work for MI6 in Greece, making journeys to the north from where he could look across the border into the country he loved and knew so well but could no longer visit. Up until his death in 1985, the same year as Hoxha, he continued to help the expatriate Albanian community, much of the time as Secretary of the Anglo-Albanian Association, which was started by Aubrey Herbert in 1918. Edith Durham had been another active member and the close connection between Britain and Albania continues today with much goodwill on both sides.

It was Aubrey Herbert of all Englishmen who did most for Albania, and if he had not died so tragically at the age of forty-three, he would have done more. In truth he was even more exceptional in real life than in the fiction of John Buchan. He seems to have been naturally fearless; at school at Eton and later at Oxford, where he gained a First in Modern History, he achieved notoriety for 'night climbing' over perilous roofs. His father, the 4th Earl of Carnarvon, who was Colonial Secretary in the ministries of Lord Derby and Disraeli (both of whom played their part in Albania's history), was later Lord Lieutenant of Ireland. Aubrey Herbert first visited Albania in 1907 and he compared it then, when it was still part of the Ottoman Empire, to Ireland.

> These two small countries are poor, while the Empires to which they belonged are rich; they begin with a bog and end with a slum; they are inhabited by people whose history is the history of factions, whose private quarrels give rise to civil war and whose creeds are conflicting. In both cases they have contributed something to the larger unit, sometimes acting as cement and sometimes as dynamite; they have hurt and they have helped.

He goes on to enumerate the ways in which both have given their overlords some of their best soldiers, brought about significant reforms and then nearly ruined them through rebellion. The price, he affirms, has been the extreme poverty of both. 'We will have no roads,' said the Albanians, 'in our country, for roads mean conquest and exploitation and disinheritance.' In the twenty-first century, Ireland has at last achieved prosperity. It cannot be long before Albania does so too, but in the meanwhile the continuing poor state of the roads suited us well.

Herbert fell in love with the people and the place immediately

> . . . for they have a charm that is their own, and their land has an almost magical attraction that leaves a permanent impression upon the majority of those who have been there. It is to be felt in the aromatic sun-scorched high-lands of the Catholic north, in the peaceful plains of the south and in the mountains beyond that sweep up to the towering crags of the Pindus and Acroceraunian ranges . . . The women have a loveliness unshared by, and different to, any other race. They look like Madonnas who have come down from snow mountains, but the wit and mental dexterity of the men of the mountains enliven the austere beauty of their women.

He describes the country as:

> . . . beautiful as a dream, that has in it the hint of a dragon . . . Everywhere gorges flung water headlong into the valleys, and so clear was the air that the farthest boundaries were as clean-cut as the impression on a coin. Though we were not riding on dizzy heights the path was dangerous; often for fifty yards at a time it was only a foot or eighteen inches broad, and sometimes frayed on the turn of a corner for a few inches into invisibility. It was impossible to dismount, and one could only watch the stones falling from the path down to where one's shadow lay sixty or a hundred feet below. I left the entire responsibility to my horse. Once it was stung by a fly, and it pranced in a way that made me tremble, but I did not touch the reins. It was a fearful joy to look ahead and mark the cliff we were to climb, where the track seemed to have had as much purchase on the face of the mountain as the shadow of a rope. It appeared impossible for horses to keep their footing upon what was only a scratch upon precipices, but they did so . . . Finally we came out on to an open hill-side covered with heather, and found one shepherd asleep amongst wild hyacinth, in the shadow of an ilex with his gun for a pillow, while his companion played upon the flute of Pan.

One of the more remarkable things about Aubrey Herbert was that he achieved all that he did in life in spite of being nearly blind. When, after the end of the First World War, he did eventually become completely blind, he was given the appalling advice that having most of his teeth extracted would restore his sight. The resulting blood poisoning killed him.

By late afternoon, we had reached the pass, where we came upon an abandoned chrome mine. Chrome used to be one of Albania's chief exports, indeed it was once the world's second-largest exporter of it, but this mine was now a sad, empty jumble of derelict buildings, rusting gantries and creaking overhead rails. There was not a soul about as we clattered through the ghostly factory. Beyond lay the small town of Krastë, which we hoped to ride through before nightfall and then find a friendly farm where we could graze the horses and sleep in a house or barn. Krastë was a caricature of the worst place on earth. It even made the ghastly suburb of Bulqizë look relatively civilised. We were reminded of Mostar in Bosnia, which we had visited soon after the heavy fighting there in 1993 and where virtually every building was ruined and riddled with bullet holes. The famed arched Ottoman bridge, built in 1566, had been destroyed, but has since been rebuilt. Here in Krastë there were no bullet holes, just neglect and decay, with an occasional furtive figure glimpsed in the shadows. It felt peculiar riding past, as though we were on the film set of a Western. Most of the ruined houses had balconies hanging off the walls, bare open doorways and glassless windows, but one had a shop on the ground floor. We stopped, and leaving Louella to hold the horses, I went in to buy a bottle of water, as there had been none of the usual roadside springs on our way up. Water they had, but very little else, just some small potatoes and pots and pans. I could see nothing to buy to feed us that evening.

I was paying for the water when a voice behind me asked, in perfect English, 'Can I help you?' I was greatly surprised, as this was the first good English I had heard from an Albanian since we started riding, much better than Mario's. He introduced himself as Tori and told us he had worked for ten years as a chef in London. Now he ran a restaurant in Tirana and he was about to leave for there in five minutes. When I explained what we were doing and gave him one of our fliers, he took in the situation at once. 'There is no question of your going any further tonight. You both look tired and it is a long way to the first village. You must stay in my flat here. My neighbour has a garden where you can leave the horses.' We protested that we could not accept his hospitality, especially as he was leaving. 'No problem,' he replied, 'my young brother is staying there and he will look after you. There is, of course, no question of paying anything, although perhaps the neighbours might be given something for the grass and hay they will provide.' He was another guardian angel, who whisked us to his tenement block round the corner, told the surprised neighbours exactly what to do and then showed us up to his flat on the first floor which, once he had unlocked and unbolted the substantial iron front door, proved to be a clean and tidy place with three bedrooms. He insisted we should sleep in his double bed, which had been stripped and had fresh sheets and blankets piled on the end. There was a tiled bathroom, with Turkish squat loo, a basin and a shower head. He gave us a set of keys and, as he was leaving, his equally surprised fifteen-year-old brother arrived and was instructed to look after us. Then he was gone.

The neighbours, who lived in the basement, were the only other occupants of the building, which was as run down as any other in Krastë, covered in graffiti and with piles of rubbish on every side. We were shown the patch where the horses could stay by the mother of the family, a large, bossy woman, who had a rather dim-witted husband and a very pretty little daughter of about eleven. There was a small square of grass surrounded by beds of pumpkins and cultivated vegetables, arranged around a traditional haystack built round a pole. We were worried the horses would eat the vegetables, but everyone seemed happy when we tied them to a fence over which grew a vine with some grapes and brought them armfuls of hay. The next morning they had eaten all the grapes as well as the hay, but they had not escaped.

We went for a walk into town once we had settled in to the apartment. The main street was beginning to show signs of life now that it was dark and there was even a café with tables outside and some men drinking. We ordered tea and a beer. To our astonishment, we were again approached by someone speaking in perfect English. This time it was a good-looking young man of about twenty-one, whose aunt owned the café. His name was Ervin and he was on holiday from Barking where he, too, worked as a chef. He had been sent to school in Dagenham by his father, who had worked in the chrome mine, and he told us that he had a degree in technical music and acting. Like Tori, whom he didn't know, he professed to love Krastë and was distressed at its decline over the last decade since the mine had closed. There had once been a thousand families living here; now there are only 150. As we spoke, the high point of Krastë's day was taking place on the street opposite us: the evening promenade. A few shabbily dressed old men and a couple of out-of-work young ones ambled about, but not a single woman walked past. When the men met, they shook hands and kissed each

Chapter 10

Mules, Mountains and Dropping Zones

We had been assured in Krastë that the track to Bizë was easy, would take three hours and we would have no problem following it. We had by now learned to be suspicious of such well-meaning advice and so left six hours. We would never have found the way without the luck of falling in with some helpful muleteers, who took us on a serious detour round the mountain ahead, not over the top where we had been advised the path led, a path which the muleteers assured us did not exist.

At first we followed a much-used goat track out of town. This took us down a sheer hillside and we had to lead the horses for a long way until we reached the bottom of a deep canyon, where there was a bridge. We crossed and started to climb through farming country, passing a couple of hamlets, but still on a good track. And it was at the second place, Bricaj, that we ran into a family group heading off on their mules to fetch firewood. The women, a mother and daughter, and two of her three sons were riding their mules, sitting sideways, which always looks so precarious but must be more comfortable than riding astride on the wooden frames. The others walked.

Here, the women all wore baggy Turkish trousers and the mother had her head covered by a white headscarf, but the daughter was bareheaded and extremely pretty and vivacious. They insisted that it was impossible to get to Bizë by continuing straight ahead over the mountain pass and indicated that we should accompany them. Life now became wonderfully easy.

They were a merry bunch, chattering away among themselves and grinning at us, unbothered by our lack of Albanian. They thought our flier was hysterical. Our horses were stimulated by the company of the mules into trotting at the same speed, as though they found it demeaning to go slower than their inferior cousins. We entered some of the most bucolic scenery we had yet seen. It is hard not to overuse this word in Albania – so much is still unspoilt and genuinely rural. Most animals are driven out to pasture each day and back again in the evening. In the remote high meadows, through which we often passed on our route down through the country, the shepherds would sleep out in shelters with their flock during the summer months. The silence of these empty landscapes was broken only by the distant tinkling of bells, deep for cows, higher toned for sheep and goats. If we were spotted, large dogs guarding and herding their flock would start to bark and if we came close they would often charge us aggressively and have to be driven off. Many of them wore rather frightening-looking iron collars with spikes to protect them in fights with wolves. The finest specimens would have been members of the ancient Molossian breed, mastiffs whose history is as old as that of any dog. One source I found on the web states that they are indigenous to the Balkans, having been bred there since Neolithic times to guard sheep since the days when both were first domesticated. Another suggests that their origins lie in Tibet, with a record of a Tibetan mastiff being given to the Emperor of China in 1121 BC, from whence they were gradually introduced to the West by nomadic herders. Whatever their origins, they are prized for their protectiveness towards their flocks and their owners. It was illegal to export them until the 1970s, when the first puppy was sent to the USA. Known as Illyrian Shepherds or Sharplaninecs, they are now bred internationally.

Now that we were with locals our reception was much more friendly and, for a time, we could ride at the same speed as the flocks we overtook, chatting to the shepherd. On either side of the wide track lay grassy alpine meadows, often with fruiting plum trees growing in the hedges. As we passed one field, the flock of sheep accompanying us suddenly charged off towards

A defensive tower – *kula* – in the Shala Valley. Men often lived in these to escape from blood-feuds.

Top: Near the top of the *Qafa e Valbonës* above the Shala Valley.
Bottom: Crossing some dangerous scree. The path was often no more than 4 inches wide.

The church in Deçani Monastery, Kosovo. A Romanesque gem, built between 1327 and 1335.

Top Left: Louella crossing the suspension bridge over the River Mollës.

Bottom Left: Louella looking across the gorge beyond Krastë at dawn.

Below: The muleteers who showed us the way to Bisë.

Crossing the Shkumbin River below a sixteenth-century Ottoman bridge, near Golik

Nico, our best guide, on his mule, Ruska. He thrummed the mule's sides with his heels and held bunches of leafy beech twigs, with which he fed her.

Portrait of Lord Byron in his Albanian costume by Thomas Phillips, 1813. The original hangs in the British Embassy in Athens. This copy hangs in the National Portrait Gallery.

the far side. There, they jostled each other below a tree which had just shed its bounteous load of purple plums, gobbling them down greedily.

The backdrop to the landscape was a range of romantic mountains and we were climbing all the time. When going up steep, rugged stretches, the mules continued at the same brisk pace but we would dismount to favour our animals. The daughter was upset by this and kept offering her mule to Louella. Why walk when you could ride? For two hours we rode together and for once I could relax, putting map and compass aside. We had deduced from their eagerness at the mention of Bizë that they were on the way there, too, but we were mistaken. At a grassy saddle high in the hills, surrounded by mature forest, which would soon provide the firewood they had come for, they revealed that our paths separated and they tried to give us directions with much arm waving. As we plainly didn't understand and it was a bit complicated, the oldest boy, who was now walking, turfed his mother off her mule and rode with us for another half hour. We would have gone wrong without him as we had to nego-tiate yet another pass and two more lay ahead, but eventually he was satisfied that we knew the way and he left us. With difficulty I persuaded him to accept 200 leka.

On our own, the tiredness from which all four of us, horses and riders alike, were suffering started to kick in and time dragged as we struggled on. Now we were following a muddy track through ancient beech woods and their smooth boles, the soft gloom, the deep shadows and the silence hushed our talk and should have brought contentment. But the ground dropped away to the bottom of yet another deep gorge where there was a narrow wooden bridge, followed by a grinding climb back up again. Our backs ached from carrying the rucksacks and my horse, Semi, had an annoying habit which made mine worse. Several times in an hour, he would stop suddenly, usually just as I had scrambled up a bank and was dragging him up behind me. Most of the time this was because he needed to defecate, which he did with astonishing frequency (we couldn't understand where he got it all from, as we were hardly overfeeding him and Louella's horse almost never went); sometimes he just stopped for no reason, wrenching my arm almost out of its socket and making me curse.

Finally, after a couple of hours, we came over one last ridge and there below us lay the plain of Bizë. On the lonely upland the air was fresh and sharp and blew coolingly on us. The head man in Fushë Bulqizë had told us that there was a Bektashi *tekke* or hermitage nearby, where we could stay or rest, and he had given us a letter to the *baba*. This was where we had arranged to meet the truck. The bare, grassy expanse stretched for several kilometres in all directions to the surrounding hills. There was not a building to be seen. We rode down and out into the plain, across which a network of tracks ran, but still no sign of human habitation. Far away to our left I spotted a flock of sheep and then, near it, a man on a horse riding off to the west. 'If we hurry', I told Louella, 'we can intercept him', and we urged our exhausted horses into a trot. We even cantered briefly in our effort to catch him and did so just as he was crossing a stone bridge over a stream, which ran through the middle of the plain. *'Ku është Bizë?'* I asked him urgently, 'Where is Bizë?' 'This is Bizë!' he replied with a laugh and, when I expressed astonishment, he said that everyone had left and no one lived here any more. I asked where the *tekke* was and he pointed back the way we had come, indicating that it would take an hour to get there. Looking back, we could now see something which had been completely hidden by a low hill. A huge, but seemingly abandoned, military base crouched like a sinister monster not far from the path we had ridden down from the pass. Rows of Nissen huts and windowless concrete buildings were clustered together, the size of a small village, but there was no sign of life or of any domestic buildings anywhere. During the Second World War, the British mission HQ had been based near Bisë and the plain was used as one of the main dropping zones for parachuting SOE operatives in to join the partisans. Now it is empty and deserted, although I have heard that it is still used for exercises by the Albanian Special Forces.

Kestrels and buzzards wheeled overhead, and far above there was a tiny speck, like hope, of an eagle. It was from the same sky that sixty-three years earlier, on 19 April 1944, three young Englishmen had parachuted into this valley. Two were Old Etonians who went on to become distinguished Conservative MPs. Julian Amery, son of Leo Amery, Secretary of State for India and one of Winston Churchill's closest friends, had a notorious elder brother, John, who was later hanged for treason. Julian served as an MP until 1992, when he was created a Life Peer.

Billy McLean, a tough and brilliant Highlander, was later to represent Inverness from 1952 to 1964. At that time, like the others, he was in his mid-twenties. Xan Fielding, in his biography, describes him as

> . . . a human epitome of cavalry dash and swagger, even though he had long ago exchanged his steed for a parachute. He was tall and slim, fair-haired and debonair, languid to the point of indolence, with conventional good looks that were far above the average and an elegance that stopped short of foppishness. But, as I soon discovered, this charming and lackadaisical façade concealed a toughness of steel, great powers of physical endurance, and a needle-sharp intelligence.

Hoxha, with whom McLean was to spend more time than he wished, remarked on his 'intelligent blue eyes, with the look of a savage cat about them'. McLean in turn said that Hoxha was fat and had a flabby handshake.

There was snow on the ground at that time, up to five feet deep in drifts, which was lucky, as they landed heavily, having been given the wrong sort of parachutes: cotton ones, only used for dropping supplies. The snow was grey on top, being covered in ash from a major eruption of Mt Vesuvius in Italy, which had occurred the month before. That eruption had destroyed, among other things, all eighty-eight planes in a US B-25 bomber group stationed near the mountain.

Their SOE mission was to reorganise the considerable number of British Liaison Officers who were operating in the area with various bands of guerillas and to persuade the surrounding tribes to take up arms against the Germans. One of the difficulties they faced in doing this was that the Germans had, in 1941, joined Kosovo to Albania and this was very popular with the northern tribes. By working with the communists, the British hoped to persuade Tito to agree that, after the war, the Kosovars would be allowed to decide their own future. Of course, it didn't work out that way, which is why there are still grave problems today. If Lord Fitzmaurice, Aubrey Herbert and Edith Durham, all of whom campaigned for a larger Albania to include all Kosovo, had been listened to, much subsequent trouble might have been avoided.

The third parachutist was David Smiley, younger son of a baronet and an expert with explosives. He knew the place well already, having chosen it as a suitable dropping zone some six months before, during his previous stint behind enemy lines. He is the only survivor today and we went to see him and his wife, Moy, on our return. Joanna Lumley, who was interviewing him for the film about our trip, came too. A sprightly ninety-one, he had gone on to have many other adventures in the Far East and in Oman, as well as commanding the Household Cavalry. He was awarded the Military Cross and bar for his activities in Albania. He told us about the legendary Fanny Hasluck, an elderly anthropologist, widow of an eminent archeologist, who had spent twenty years in Albania before the war and wrote the definitive book on blood-feuds: *Unwritten Law in Albania*. The Italians had expelled her as a spy in 1939 and since then she had run, at first single-handedly, the Albanian section of SOE in Cairo. An unlikely Head of Section, she claimed to have smuggled messages between Athens and London in her garters, when working for British Intelligence during the First World War. In Cairo she was described as 'the only person in the Middle East with a knowledge of the Albanian language, Albania and the Albanians'. Smiley describes her in his book, *Albanian Assignment*, as having 'greying hair swept back into a bun and a pink complexion with bright blue eyes; she reminded me of an old-fashioned English nanny. Full of energy and enthusiasm, she was totally dedicated to her beloved Albania.' All her 'boys', whom she briefed on the country and taught Albanian, adored her. She taught them Albanian nursery rhymes, which came in surprisingly useful on odd occasions as ice-breakers, and often sent them signals in the field directing them to nearby beauty spots 'where they could enjoy a picnic'. On his first assignment Smiley had a mule for several months of which he became very fond and which he called Fanny. 'I used to kiss her on the nose,' he said, and it reminded me of how we used to kiss our gentle Albanian horses. When relieved for a time, he left Fanny with his successor, Alan Hare, who was also in the Household Cavalry. On his return he was devastated to find that Fanny had been eaten during a particularly severe winter. 'I told him that cavalry officers don't eat mules!' He paused and looked thoughtful. 'Actually, mules are OK and I've eaten plenty of them – and I ate an Italian once, too. After Italy surrendered in September 1943, the Italians were in disarray and those who ran away were starving. There were dead and dying troops all along the roads, but I bumped into some officers who had got themselves quite well organised and set up a good camp. I dined with them on an excellent stew, rather peppery. When I had finished, their colonel asked me if I had enjoyed it. I asked whether it was horse or mule – all the sheep and cows had, of course, been eaten by then. "Oh no!" he replied, "that was Giuseppe, our Mess Waiter!"'

David Smiley also told us the astonishing story of the thirteen American nurses, whose plane crash-landed near Berat on 8 November 1943. A Dakota C53 on a routine flight from Sicily to Bari in Italy managed to get so lost that it ran out of fuel over Albania. On board were the two pilots, fifteen enlisted men and thirteen pretty young nurses, second lieutenants in a Medivac unit. To avoid it falling into the hands of the Germans, who were all around, they burnt the aircraft and headed into the mountains, where they were picked up by partisans who billeted them in peasant houses. 'All the SOE officers made a beeline to get to them, but Lieutenant Gavin Duffy got there first, lucky devil!' Smiley said. He was ordered to arrange their evacuation. For the next six weeks they had a terrible time, being strafed and dive-bombed by German planes and having to walk for hours each day. President Roosevelt heard about their plight and arranged a parachute supply-drop of cosmetics and silk stockings, which must have cheered them up, but they were becoming tired and ill with dysentery and jaundice. Corporal Willie

Williamson, who was attached to them to help with their evacuation, described them as 'the finest women I ever met. They walked for miles, powdered their faces and were so smart.' On 29 December, an evacuation was attempted from the airfield at Girokaster. A Wellington bomber, two Dakotas and thirty-six Lightning Fighters circled the field for nearly an hour, while the nurses huddled in a ditch and a German armoured unit covered them with their guns from the far side. Lt Duffy decided it was too dangerous for the planes to land and sent them away to the accompaniment of the girls' cries. The weary party struggled on to the coast, where they arrived in poor shape but in high spirits. They spent the night of 8 January 1944 in a cave, code-named Seaview, which was occupied by Major Anthony Quayle who went on to star in the film *The Guns of Navarone*. They were fed on eggs and bacon, suckling-pig, strong red wine, brandy, chocolate and coffee. No scene in any war film can have compared with the strangeness of that real one. They were picked up early the next morning by a high-speed motor gunboat, which delivered them safely back to Bari.

Anthony Quayle ran Seaview for three months. It was a long low cave in which goats and sheep had previously been kept, with the result that it was infested with lice and also scorpions. There was no water there, so that those in residence had to drink from rainwater puddles. But it was at the end of a dog-legged creek between steep cliffs and with a little beach, which was ideal for evacuating people in calm weather. Soon after the nurses passed through, Quayle had a meeting with the Ballist commander, who warned him what would happen if the Allies went on supporting the communists. The Balli Kombëtar, known as Ballists, were the fiercely anti-communist nationalist resistance movement. They were also republicans and totally opposed to the return of King Zog. The fascist tyranny, he said, would be replaced by an equally appalling communist tyranny, which would sweep over the whole of the Balkans. Quayle fought bravely and took many risks dodging German troops who were searching for his hideout. He lost several mules, not to enemy action, but to wolves.

Later, David Smiley recalls visiting Quayle in hospital in Bari, where he had been evacuated suffering from malaria, jaundice and dysentery at the same time and looking 'pretty ill'. In *The Guns of Navarone*, made eighteen years later, there is a scene in which he is seen lying on a stretcher. Smiley says he looked 'just the same'!

During a leave in January 1944, Smiley, Amery and McLean had a meeting with Anthony Eden, the Foreign Secretary, and it was he who decided that all three should be parachuted back into the north of the country. Later, McLean was to write to Eden to tell him what was going on, but his letter was intercepted and never reached him. They also met the exiled King Zog who, after a time living in the Ritz, then had a grand house in Buckinghamshire called Parmoor. He still had the red Mercedes that Hitler had given him. It had saved his life when he was fleeing Paris just ahead of the invading Germans in 1940. Because it was an exact replica of the Führer's own car, the Luftwaffe pilot who strafed the convoy of cars in which the royal party was travelling had stopped shooting when he saw it. Eventually, Zog gave it to the Red Cross. He was passionately anti-communist and even then he was warning Churchill and Roosevelt that communism posed an even greater danger than the Nazis, but their priority was to win the war with Germany at all costs. His wife, Queen Geraldine, became a special friend of Smiley's and was, he said, a delightful person. They corresponded a lot and she assuredly loved these brave young men risking their lives for her country, to which she was never to return. She called Amery, McLean and Smiley her three musketeers. To their considerable embarrassment, McLean and Smiley were also given the codenames 'Paste' and 'Grin', puns which they made clear they did not choose themselves!

Back in Albania that summer, they received occasional airdrops of useful things and even some luxuries. Smiley had *The Tatler*, *Picture Post* and *Horse and Hound* dropped in a special container, as well as occasional copies of *The Times* and even the odd bottle of whisky. But there were dangerous moments, too, and they had thrilling adventures dodging the Germans, who tried hard to catch them. 'Once', he told Joanna, 'I was running away from them when I came on a meadow of simply delicious wild strawberries. I stopped to pick some and had to hoof it over the hill fast when they came out of the woods and started shooting at me. When I got to the top, I looked back and saw that they had all stopped and were gathering strawberries themselves!'

'You treat it all so lightly, but it must have been pretty awful most of the time?' Joanna Lumley asked. 'Well, it wasn't always very nice', he replied with a gentle smile. And then he began to open up, not about his own sufferings, but about how dreadful it had really been for the Albanians and how badly we had let them down. He had kept meticulous scrapbooks of his two tours of duty in Albania, in which the names of the thirty-odd British officers who were parachuted in, as well as the Albanians alongside whom they fought, were recorded beside the still-sharp black-and-white photographs taken with his little Leica. The originals are now in the Imperial War Museum. During his first tour in 1943, they were mostly with the communist partisans, who were better organised. But they soon realised that the communists' objective was to save themselves so as to be in a strong position to take over once the war was over. They seldom went into action, but sent out by radio glowing reports of spurious victories, and the British, who were supplying them with arms, fell for their stories. Meanwhile, the nationalists, the Balli Kombëtar, and the Legality Movement – royalist supporters of King Zog – were doing most of the fighting, but getting little or no thanks, recognition – or arms. By the time of Smiley's second assignment in 1944, civil war had broken out between the communists and the rest. He and his colleagues continued to fight with those prepared to die for their country, and kept telling their HQ, now in Bari, what was really going on. This infuriated the communists, who were now being led by Enver Hoxha, to the extent that they put a price on the heads of the British, forcing them to flee. The British wanted to take some of the courageous leaders they had fought with out to safety, since they knew they would be massacred by the communists if left behind, and they repeatedly radioed their HQ to explain the situation. But at that time their bosses were heavily infiltrated by our own communist sympathisers, who refused to listen and concentrated on keeping the Russians, who were still our allies, happy, although the Russians never did anything to help the partisans. As a result, a naval officer was even sent with the two boats which eventually evacuated the British to make sure no Albanians were let on board, although there was plenty of room for them. All this was done specifically so as not to annoy Enver Hoxha and Smiley describes it as one of the saddest moments of his life.

It was a terrible betrayal and, as Smiley wrote in his book, had British aid gone the other way, Albania would have become a pro-western democracy. But worse was to come. After the war, for three years between 1948 and 1951, the US and the UK trained and equipped hundreds of expatriate Albanians and infiltrated them back into the country. Having realised their ghastly mistake in backing the wrong side, hearing about the appalling purges being carried out by Hoxha and believing that many Albanians were ready to rise up against him, they decided that this was the perfect place to give Stalin a bloody nose and to show that communism was not unstoppable. (Strangely enough, in 1917, when Albania was occupied by the Austrians, the Albanians of America had tried to persuade the British government to help them invade their homeland. They offered to raise a brigade of 3,000 to 4,000 men and put themselves under the command of Aubrey Herbert!) In 1948, Czechoslovakia was taken over by the communists and in the same year Tito was thrown out of the Cominform, thus cutting Albania off from the rest of the Soviet bloc. Apart from the potential propaganda impact which success would bring, information had been received that Russia was promising Albania aid in return for the right to build a naval base at Valona on the Adriatic. The prospect of Russian submarines being able to operate freely in the heart of the Mediterranean gave further impetus to the plan and Ernest Bevin, the Foreign Secretary, authorised the use of covert action to detach Albania from the Soviet orbit. With the exception of the equally disastrous Bay of Pigs episode in Cuba in 1961, this was the only time in the whole of the Cold War when a serious effort was made to invade and overthrow a communist country. The landings, which took place both by sea and air, were organised by David Smiley in Malta. It was a top-secret operation and it is still not widely known about – and it should have been successful. Time and again, groups of heavily armed men, with a couple of radios and trained in using codes, were parachuted near the villages they came from, with instructions to mobilise the resistance they were assured they would find to the hated regime. Others were put ashore from fishing boats commanded by British officers disguised as Greek fishermen. Time and again, they were caught almost immediately, to be tortured to the verge of insanity before being paraded at show trials in Tirana and either shot or condemned to hard labour for life. Their relations and neighbours were also tortured and massacred in large numbers. As one of the few to escape, Halil Nerguti, said later:

> We knew that they would retaliate against our families. In fact they did against my family. They shot my brother Hysen and my father died in one of their camps. But our eyes were open about this and we had to do what we did. It was the right moment. There were internal quarrels in Albania at that time, the Yugoslavs were out and the Russians were not fully in control. So it was realistic and we had high hopes. Unfortunately, we were betrayed.

Something was dreadfully wrong. It was not until 25 May 1951, when Burgess and Maclean fled from England, that the penny began to drop. The British had a highly placed spy in their midst, who was tipping off the Russians about each infiltration. Kim Philby, officially First Secretary at the British Embassy in Washington but really one of Britain's intelligence representative in the USA, was the link between the British and the American intelligence agencies. Guy Burgess had been living with him and a few days after his defection, Philby was recalled to London. MI5's top men were convinced he was guilty and an internal trial concluded that he probably was, but there was not sufficient evidence to convict him. Amazingly, he was merely sacked from the secret service with a golden handshake of £4,000 and given lowly jobs, about which he and some of his many friends complained loudly. They believed he was a victim of the rampant McCarthyism of the day. As a result, although he was a pariah to some, he spent much of his time lunching at his clubs (I am glad that my own, The Travellers, was not one of them) with serving members of the service, who commiserated with him and probably revealed much of what they were doing, so that he was still able to be useful to Moscow. It was to be another twelve years before he finally defected, while in Lebanon. 'The plain fact', said Moy Smiley later, 'is that he was a cold-blooded killer!' and for an instant, in the face of that sweet lady, I saw the fury which is still felt by many at his treachery.

All Europe suffered from this fiasco for almost forty years. It has remained one of the most carefully concealed secrets of the Cold War, which neither side chose to reveal. It was a humiliating operational disaster for the West, whereas in the communist sphere news that infiltration had taken place would have sent out all the wrong messages. If it had succeeded, and but for Kim Philby it well might have done so, underground movements throughout the new communist empire would have taken comfort. They would have seen that revolt against their masters was possible and that the West could and would help them. The Cold War might well have been radically curtailed. But it was the Albanians who suffered worst from our failures. Enver Hoxha was confirmed in his paranoia that the West was about to invade him – because it had been ready to do just that. He built 750,000 concrete bunkers to repel the enemy, wasting his country's sparse resources in the effort and diverting attention from the many other problems it faced. For forty years he ruled the most extreme communist country of all, 'more Stalinist than Stalin himself', banning all private ownership, abolishing religion, keeping a large proportion of his people in labour camps and becoming the world's longest-surviving dictator. Again and again in his speeches he justified his policies by referring to the American and British 'invasion'.

As I have researched Albania's history and read some of the large body of writings about those dreadful days, I have come to share my country's guilt and to believe that we owe a huge debt to the wild Albanians, who fought so bravely at our side during the Second World War and who, since the time of Byron, had looked on the British as exemplars of honour. Halil that the scenery was as rugged and spectacular as ever. We were glad that we didn't have to find a way through it on horseback as the southern escarpment of the mountains looked dangerously steep. We dropped off the horses at Bujar's farm outside the town and went on to the Wakeleys' base. There we met Nick's wife, Sar, who generously allowed us to completely unload the Landcruiser and so take up most of the available space around their courtyard. We sat in the evening sun with them over a welcome cup of tea and discussed the complicated plans we would need to make over the next couple of days if we were to complete our journey. Nick knew an acclaimed horse vet, who would examine our two the next day and advise us on whether they were fit to continue. We were pretty sure Chris would not be able to go on. Her saddle sore was getting worse and although it was not troubling her yet, she was going slower and slower through sheer exhaustion.

Ylly and Durim soon joined us and it was wonderful to have Nick translate fluently between us, so that we could explain what we planned and what the problems were. When the saddle sore was mentioned, they rummaged around in the heap of baggage we had unloaded from our roof rack and returned with two large bundles wrapped in white sacking. We had noticed these but thought them part of their personal kit, as they were stitched up. Now they unwrapped them and took out two saddles. 'If you had used Chris's own saddle, this one here, she would not have developed a sore,' they said through Nick. At that moment I could have killed them both. From the first day, when we had tried out our saddles and bridles and they had helped us, and throughout our daily travails, they had never mentioned the existence of these saddles. 'Why didn't you tell us you had them?' we asked. 'You never asked,' they replied.

Nick had booked us into the best hotel in Elbasan, the Real Scampis, named after the ancient Roman city of Scampis, which was set beside the Via Egnatia. This strategic highway was constructed in the second century BC in order to link the chain of Roman colonies stretching towards the Bosphorus. The Via Appia, along which the armies of Julius Caesar and Pompey marched, led from Rome to Brindisi (Brundisium), a point almost exactly opposite the start of the Via Egnatia, across the Adriatic at Durres (Dyrrachium). One of the ancient world's great military and trade routes, the Via Egnatia played a fundamental part in the spread of Christianity, as many of the crusading armies travelled that way to Constantinople. It divides Albania in half. Elbasan, which means 'strong place' in Turkish, was built by the Ottoman invaders in the fifteenth century and remained a tranquil and delightful town until the Second World War, when it was much damaged. Then Hoxha, with Chinese assistance, built a giant steel factory, called The Mao Tse-Tung Metallurgical Complex, which polluted the whole valley but which is now, thankfully, just an empty shell.

The hotel, built inside the massive ramparts of the fifteenth-century Ottoman walls, was comfortable and we revelled in hot water, clean towels and the prospect of an excellent dinner. The dish of the day was 'Real Scampis Special' and Louella ordered it, salivating at the prospect of some seafood, only to be disappointed by the arrival of a now all-too-familiar meat stew named here after the Roman city.

We were half way through our journey. Time to pause and look back at the wild and still untamed country we had made our way through before entering the hotter, southern land ahead, where different, more cultured literary and historical delights awaited us, we hoped.

PART III

Lear Country

Chapter 11

Across the Via Egnatia

Edward Lear rode into Albania from Lake Ochrid and Macedonia on 24 September 1848, following the Shkumbin River to Elbasan. He painted some of his finest pictures in Albania and rode all over the western part of the country. He found the landscape perfectly suited to his temperament and wrote of it as

> . . . realising the fondest fancies of artist imagination! The wide branching oak, firmly rivetted in crevices, all tangled over with fern and creepers, hung halfway down the precipice of a giant crag, while silver-white goats (which chime so picturesquely in with such landscapes as this) stood motionless as statues on the highest pinnacle, sharply defined against the clear blue sky. Here and there the broken foreground of rocks piled on rocks, was enlivened by some Albanians who toiled upwards, now shadowed by spreading beeches, now glittering in the bright sun on slopes of the greenest lawn, studded over with tufted trees, which recalled Stothard's [Thomas Stothard 1755–1834, English painter and engraver and friend of William Blake] graceful forms, so knit with my earliest ideas of landscape.

He goes on to describe how difficult he found it to turn away from

> . . . this magnificent mountain view – from these chosen nooks and corners of a beautiful world – from sights of which no painter-soul can ever weary:

even now, that fold beyond fold of wood, swelling far as the eye can reach – that vale ever parted by its serpentine river – that calm blue plain, with Tomhor in the midst, like an azure island in a boundless sea, haunt my mind's eye and vary the present with visions of the past.

Lear was a most unlikely but extremely brave traveller. Short-sighted, prone to innumerable illnesses, a hopeless horseman, Susan Hyman in *Edward Lear in the Levant* described him as 'terrified of dogs, horses and firearms, prone to severe seasickness and driven to distraction by noise and disorder'. Yet he travelled alone, except for his faithful Albanian 'dragoman, cook valet, interpreter, and guide' Giorgio Kokali, and far more lightly than most other explorers of the time, through some of the most exotic and dangerous regions of his day and often where no Englishman had yet been. Kokali, who was to stay with Lear for the rest of his life and who was buried with him at San Remo where they both died, was, according to his master, 'a semi-civilised Suliot, much like wild Rob Roy'. Lear's description of himself, in a poem written twenty-three years later, was:

> How pleasant to know Mr Lear!
> Who has written such volumes of stuff!
> Some think him ill-tempered and queer,
> But a few think him pleasant enough.
>
> His mind is concrete and fastidious,
> His nose is remarkably big;
> His visage is more or less hideous,
> His beard it resembles a wig.

Lear's best artistic work was done in 1848–9 during his tour of Greece and Albania, and his painting and writing from that period are regarded as outstanding records of those vanished times and scenes. He was also a fine ornithological draughtsman and his lithographs of birds, especially parrots, have been compared to the best work of Audubon. Lord Stanley, later the 14th Earl of Derby, three times Prime Minister and the longest-serving leader of the Conservative party, became one of his patrons and invited him to draw his aviary at Knowsley Hall. There is a nice story about this, which may be apocryphal, but has the ring of truth. Lord and Lady Stanley were undecided as to where Lear should eat. It seemed wrong to condemn him to the servants' hall and yet he was not quite a gentleman and so could not really dine with them. 'I know,' Lady Stanley is reputed to have said. 'He can go up to the nursery. The children seem to like him!' And so his best-known talent of creating nonsense rhymes was honed as he enchanted the children and painted parrots. An odd coincidence here is that Disraeli, who also had Albanian connections, as we have seen, served under Lord Derby before taking over as Prime Minister himself. They must all have spoken of Albania from time to time.

While Mickey happily ensconced himself in Elbasan's excellent Internet Café and uploaded lots of film onto our website, we set about sorting out the problems with our horses, at least one of which was not in a fit state to continue. Nick's vet friend, Pirro Kota, was more than we could have hoped for. One of Albania's top vets and a fine horseman in his day, he calmly set about finding solutions. First, he took us to a café on the edge of town where there were two young bay stallions. They hadn't been ridden for a month and looked a bit wild, but they were a possibility. Their owner wasn't there and while we waited we were introduced to a young man called Jeton Çekrezi, Tony for short, who said he had a horse. He was extremely good looking – like an Italian film star, Louella said – and there was a stillness and earnestness about him which made us both want to see the horse. He jumped on his moped and led us a mile down the main road and into a vast, desolate industrial complex. Once it had been a part of the steel factory, but now weeds grew everywhere among the ruined buildings and potholed roads, while sheep grazed between the piles of litter. Leaving us, Tony scooted off across country towards some giant sheds, over which towered a factory chimney. We waited. Suddenly a lovely black mare galloped out of the bushes straight towards us; it was like a scene from *Black Beauty*. She did not look as though she was going to stop and my first thought was 'No way will either of us be riding that!' Near where we were standing was a water trough we had not noticed and, as we stood frozen to the spot, she skidded to a stop and started drinking. Tony arrived and started to pet her. There was manifest love on both sides.

Her name was Bora, which means 'snow' in Albanian – a joke as she was deepest black. Her mother had been shot dead by a farmer when she was five days old and she still had some pellets in her. Tony, who earned his living as a truck driver, spent everything he had on looking after her in this unlikely setting. He hoped to turn her into a show jumper and Pirro was helping him. He put a big Western saddle on her and rode her round. I tried, gingerly at first, then getting her to canter, and found her responsive and gentle. When Louella mounted, the die was cast and, if Tony would let us have her, this would be her horse from now on. He needed some persuading, as she was the centre of his life, but he agreed because, so he said, what we were doing was important for Albania. Louella promised to take the greatest care and return Bora safe and sound.

We thought it would be a good idea to see how she would get on with the stallions, if we were to choose one of them for me. To our amazement, Tony galloped Bora flat out alongside us as we drove back along the main road, weaving in and out of the heavy and fast-moving traffic. When we passed a petrol station, they shot straight through between the pumps, putting to flight the attendants filling cars. No one else appeared particularly surprised by this behaviour and we guessed that Tony and Bora were a familiar sight in that part of town.

Back at the café, Tony and I tried the stallions and I said I could manage one of them if there was no alternative, although it sweated profusely and was hard to control. Pirro was doubtful once he had examined it and having watched us ride. He said that he thought it might have a weak hind leg. We decided to take a decision after we had seen how Chris and Semi were and the next morning we drove out to Bujar's farm to see them. Pirro felt them both all over carefully and agreed that it would be unwise to ride Chris any further. He rode Semi: the first time he had ridden for seventeen years, he said. He sprayed Semi's cuts and scratches with purple antiseptic and pronounced him fit to continue. His own saddle now fitted him better and just one day and two nights of rest and good food had made a remarkable difference. I was quite happy with this decision, as although he was slow and needed constant urging, he was a brave and willing horse, who had never failed to do what I had asked of him. Perhaps, I thought, the stimulus of having the beautiful Bora as his companion might make him go faster.

While this was being decided, I mentioned to Pirro that Semi had recently been bleeding a little from the mouth which, as I rode him in a bitless bridle, seemed strange. Putting his hand inside and feeling round among the teeth, the vet immediately found the largest horse leech I have ever seen. It was black, almost as big as my thumb and firmly attached below the rear molars. Everyone sprang into action, knowing just what to do. First, salt was fetched from the farmhouse and rubbed all over the inside of Semi's mouth. After a few minutes, a lighted cigarette was applied to the leech, but neither remedy had any immediate effect. Tony now took over, manipulating the leech with his fingers and pushing it from side to side. Eventually, it dropped off. Semi must have picked it up from one of the stagnant ponds he had drunk from. Without it, he would feel even better.

In Elbasan we had both Bora and Semi re-shod. Because we would still be going over mountains and through rough and roadless country, we were advised to have special shoes fitted. They were like the crude ones on our first horses with solid plates underneath and the blacksmith, who worked out of an underground bunker in the centre of town, did a sterling job. It is a credit to Albania's blacksmiths that our horses never cast a single shoe while we were there.

Back at the hotel, we had an appointment for tea. Mark Vickers, the British Military Attaché, had driven over from Tirana to bring me a special package, which had arrived through the Diplomatic Bag. My son Rupert is a keen fisherman and he hoped that we would be able to catch a dinner of trout sometimes from the many rivers we would be crossing. Rupert had sent out his three favourite spinners and Mark was kindly delivering them. We were to pass many tempting trout rivers and occasionally we saw someone fishing. During the day I couldn't carry the rod with me and, somehow, we always camped too late for me to flog any rivers in daylight. I never did catch an Albanian fish.

I was already deeply in Mark's debt, as it was he who had come through with our excellent maps. He knew the country intimately, having travelled widely throughout it. He had just learned that the Foreign and Commonwealth Office was about to announce that the post of Military Attaché to Albania was to be axed. This seemed to us short-sighted, since Albania is likely soon to play a significant part in the geopolitics of the region. With the escalating problems in Kosovo, always ready to burst into flames again with their intention to declare independence from the Serbs, it would be useful for our government to have an ear close to the ground there. George W. Bush had recently made the first state visit of an American President to Albania, describing it as a 'staunch ally in the war on terrorism'. Soon after our return, Albania was invited to join NATO. Mark Vickers is now serving in Nepal.

Mark was also in direct contact with the Ministry of Defence and intermittently by mobile with us, so that we could be contacted rapidly if anything happened to our son, Merlin, in Afghanistan. At the time we had no idea that he had had a very near miss a couple of weeks before and that it was being kept from us.

Merlin had been deployed to the Helmand district of Afghanistan. He and his troop, who drove light Scimitar tanks, were there for six months fighting in the front line of a campaign that was widely being reported as the fiercest since the Second World War. On 30 August 2007, the day we crossed into Albania, while driving in convoy with the rest of his squadron near Sangin, Merlin's tank went over an old Soviet mine. His CO was to write later, in an article in the *Independent*:

I was in the command vehicle when 2nd Lt Merlin Hanbury-Tenison's Scimitar hit a mine north of Sangin. I felt the vibration in my chest even at 1,000 metres. I threw a glance at [my] second in command, whose face showed he also suspected we had lost the entire crew. I felt a sickening lurch of the stomach. The shouts for the ambulance started immediately and we stewed for about 10 seconds. It seemed like an age before we heard they had given a thumbs up.

The only reason Merlin and his crew survived was that they had just taken delivery of a fresh supply of Scimitars, which had been fitted for the first time with a protective metal plate underneath. Previously, when these light tanks went over a big mine the result was nearly always death or very serious injury. This was the first time the new plate had been put to the test in Afghanistan. Although the tank was destroyed and parts of it were blasted as much as 500 metres away, the crew walked away from the wreckage. Because of the intense heat – up to 50 degrees in the open and over 60 degrees inside the metal interior – they were not wearing their flack jackets, which were strapped to the outside, ready for use in the event of an ambush by the Taliban. When a helicopter was diverted to pick them up and take them back to Camp Bastion to be checked, they had to put their jackets on, since regulations required them to be worn. They found that they had been virtually shredded by the blast. Inside the helicopter were twenty young Coldstream Guardsmen on their way to their first potential encounter with the enemy. Merlin, his gunner and driver, blackened, ragged and apparently shot to pieces, were not an encouraging sight. As their hearing began to return after the blast, they enjoyed the horrified comments and the expressions on the faces of those sitting opposite them.

We had decided to recommence our journey the other side of Librazhd, where a dirt cross-country road left the main trans-Albania thoroughfare at a place called Qukës and headed south alongside the Shkumbin River. Thanks to the efficiency of Bujar, it all went like clockwork. He transported Bora and Semi in his truck and we followed. In spite of unloading all our surplus stores on the kind Wakeley family, we still did not quite have room in the Landcruiser for all of us to squeeze in, and so we hired a taxi to drive in convoy with us. By midday, we had unloaded the horses beside the road, saddled up and were on our way again.

The sun blazed down and the countryside we were now in felt different from everywhere else we had been. There are two distinct peoples in Albania: Ghegs in the north and the Tosks in the south. Each has their own dialect. Kosovor Albanians are Ghegs, who make up two-thirds of all Albanians. King Zog was a Gheg and before the Second World War the Ghegs dominated Albanian politics, but after the war many Tosks came to power because the new communist government drew most of its support from them. Enver Hoxha was a Tosk from Girokaster.

The Tosks from the south claim to be more intellectual and it is true that many politicians and leaders come from there. The Ghegs have always had a reputation for being reserved and warlike, great fighters. Skanderbeg was from a Gheg area and many of the military and the police still come from the north today. It was always thus, even under the Ottoman Empire, when the north was never fully pacified. Ghegs, who are often described as fair, are taller than Tosks, who are darker and more Mediterranean. Albanians from both parts of the country can understand each other perfectly, but will always be aware from the accent who they are talking to; just as in Britain northerners and southerners can still usually detect the other's origins.

The Via Egnatia, running alongside the Shkumbin River, represents the divide between these peoples and we were now entering Tosk country. We noticed that here the people smiled more readily. Some called out a greeting as we rode past, a few even in English. The farms looked prosperous, with tall crops shaded by poplars and acacias, and the hedgerows were laden with plums on which we gorged ourselves to such an extent that we both got tummy aches. After an hour or so of very pleasant riding, in marked contrast to the alarums and doubts of our last few days in Gheg country, we came upon the most graceful man-made object we were to see in Albania. Below us on our right across a meadow, rose a fine and terribly romantic Ottoman bridge, dripping with creepers. Like the famous bridge at Mostar in Bosnia, its arch ascended steeply towards heaven. It was narrow, without a parapet, and there was a smaller arch and 'window' on one side. Louella is fearless at times like this, but I had to nerve myself not to look down as we rode across.

Edward Lear may well have crossed this very bridge and he describes an incident on another, further downstream. 'We crossed the Skumbi, here a very formidable stream, by one of those lofty one-arched bridges so common in Turkey, and as the baggage-horse descended the last step down came the luggage once more, so that my sketches would have been lost, *sensa rimedio*, had the accident occurred two seconds sooner.'

In 1851, Lear sent his friend Alfred Lord Tennyson, who had recently become Poet Laureate, a copy of his book, *Journals of a landscape painter in Greece and Albania,* as a wedding present. In thanks, Tennyson wrote a poem for him, which captures the Albanian landscape as well as the Greek of the title.

TO E.L., ON HIS TRAVELS IN GREECE

Alfred, Lord Tennyson

Illyrian woodlands, echoing falls
Of water, sheets of summer glass,
The long divine Peneïan pass,
The vast Akrokeraunian walls,

Tomohrit, Athos, all things fair,
With such a pencil, such a pen,
You shadow forth to distant men,
I read and felt that I was there:

And trust me while I turn'd the page,
And track'd you still on classic ground,

I grew in gladness till I found
My spirits in the golden age.

For me the torrent ever pour'd
And glisten'd – here and there alone
The broad-limb'd Gods at random thrown
By fountain-urns; – and Naiads oar'd

A glimmering shoulder under gloom
Of cavern pillars; on the swell
The silver lily heaved and fell;
And many a slope was rich in bloom

From him that on the mountain lea
By dancing rivulets fed his flocks
To him who sat upon the rocks,
And fluted to the morning sea.

Our route took us further down the valley until we crossed the Shkumbin River for the last time and started to climb up into the hills again, passing many a shepherd who sat on the mountain lea by dancing rivulets and fed his flocks. For another three hours we ground on up an ever-steeper road, looking down into fertile valleys where neat crops were being harvested with the most basic of tools. An old man wrestled with a wooden plough behind two donkeys; women scythed thick grass on terraced fields and piled it into haycocks; sheaves of wheat were lined up in tidy stooks between rows of maize and cabbages. It looked idyllic, but we knew how hard the farmers' lives were, especially now so many of the young had left. At least, as a legacy of communism, virtually everyone in the country had electricity from the 'Light of the Party' hydro-electric plant in the north of the country, although that system is now breaking down. Another potential legacy of communism, which has also literally collapsed, was the terracing of steep hillsides in order to reforest them. Eric Newby, who visited Albania in 1983, right at the end of the communist era, saw 'barren, limestone foothills . . . now burgeoned with fruit trees . . . on a vast scale . . . one above the other, like contour lines. And there were enormous olive groves and vineyards, many of them so recently planted that neither had yet yielded a crop . . . many of them in very inaccessible situations.' We saw many hillsides with terracing, but very few where trees were growing. They could have been prehistoric remains, like those one sees in the Andes abandoned by earlier civilisations, and we asked what they were for. 'They were for trees,' we were told by a villager, 'but now nobody cares.' It seems that the irrigation has been allowed to lapse, so that most of the saplings have died and vanished. Newby suggests that they were planted with forced labour. Recent research in the Shala Valley, where we started, has revealed that the new terraces built under communism were often just 'make-work', to keep the people busy. The apple trees planted are still there, but they were a total failure and seldom bear fruit.

Newby also tells how there was no litter to be seen in 1983, 'partly because the Albanians had not yet learned to package merchandise for home consumption, other than screw it up in a bit of brown paper, and because chucking it about was a serious, anti-social offence. There was no dogs' mess, either, because there were no dogs . . . ' The all-pervasive litter we saw from the moment we crossed the border from Montenegro was perhaps the worst memory we have of the otherwise idyllic Albanian landscape. We sometimes wished, too, that there were fewer dogs with the shepherds and their flocks, since they were almost always savage and aggressive.

When we reached the village of Trebinje at teatime, we found our crew waiting for instructions – and no tea. 'Do I have to do everything?' I muttered crossly as I showed them where to make camp and helped them set it up. They had chosen a piece of waste ground in the middle of the village, between the cemetery and an apple orchard. It was not an ideal site and quite a distance from the nearest source of water, but it was too late to move. As we led the horses to water, we discovered Bora's only fault: she was very strong and didn't like being led slowly, especially when there was water or a meal ahead. This was the first of many times when we had to let her go and make her own way at a gallop. Once she arrived at the small spring, some way down the hill, she stopped, drank and was once again as gentle and sweet as anyone could wish. Semi was better behaved with a consistently gentle nature. They were both to stay with us for the rest of our journey and we became very fond of them.

In the evening, the local lads gathered round our camp and watched fascinated as Mickey edited the day's filming on his laptop. That night I had cramp again. For me, this had been the worst thing about the journey so far: the almost nightly 'punishment' of acute, agonising pain in both legs. The torment is almost unbearable, lasts longer than seems fair and is hard to alleviate. I found that pushing my feet against something solid helped, and our tent at the back of the Landcruiser was ideal for this. Lying on the ground in the tent, I could lift my legs up to the lowered tailgate and press with all my might. This took my mind off the pain and did, eventually, work.

That night I lay awake thinking about the next day. Soon after Trebinje, we would be leaving the road and, heading due south towards Voskopojë, winding our way over a series of passes. Our crew would be driving a long way round to the west through Pogradeç and almost to Korçë, before turning back to the east and hoping to intercept us. We badly needed a guide. I had made a preliminary attempt with the villagers and had offered one grumpy old man who said he knew the way 5,000 leka (£25) to come with us. He had immediately asked for 10,000 and I had been forced by pride as much as economy to say that we would find someone at the last village before we separated from Durim. Durim clearly disliked such negotiations and shrugged and walked away just when I needed him most. Whether he resented the exorbitant sums I was forced to offer in order to elicit any interest, whether he disliked having to deal with rustics, or whether he found the whole thing beneath him, we never found out. With his very limited English, discussion was near impossible, but he well knew what we wanted and he could have helped more. Fortunately, he was an excellent driver and mechanic and he looked after our vehicle well.

Edward Lear shames me with his enthusiasm, his eye for detail and his equanimity, even though his journey was far more arduous and beastly than ours. After yet another night in a filthy *khan* (inn), with no sleep because of the fleas and chickens in his bed and the din of pigs and cattle all around, he is able to write:

The great meadow-plains of Kaváya, bounded by low down-like hills, clothed with growth of olive trees, were most pleasant to look on; and in conse-quence of the baggage horse falling, by which all the *roba* was disarranged, one had the more time to contemplate the oxen and buffaloes without number, and the sheep and geese that enliven the wide green surface. Throughout the extent of flat country great flocks of geese are taken out to pasture every morning by a goose-herd; they are carefully watched from sunrise to sunset, for fear of vultures by day and wolves by night; and are then driven home to their respective villages, after the fashion of goats in Italy. We met many peasants, but the gay Gheghe [sic]colours are giving place to white costume . . . About three we met a bridal party – the bride being conveyed on horseback to the future husband's house; she seemed to be a strange thing, like a large doll – so closely swaddled and wrapped up that neither face nor figure were visible, while a tall sprig of rosemary, which finished off her head-dress, gave her the appearance of some exotic plant in process of careful conveyance to a gardener's ground.

Lear was further to the west of us when he wrote this almost exactly 160 years before. Since then, the people have changed and we saw few flocks of geese; but the landscape has remained unaltered and I dreamt that night of entering a more tranquil and more Mediterranean country as we headed south.

Chapter 12

Echoes of Albania's Past

The view to which we awoke was different to Lear's: more mountainous and full of trees. Poplars and aspen were just beginning to acquire their autumn hues: delicate shades of gold which shimmered in the morning breeze. Wherever there was a piece of flat land on the valley floor, neat rows of corn stooks and haycocks, interspersed with dark-green belts of cabbage, cucumber and melon, created a Toytown view, like a child's picture of how a farm should be.

The first village we came to in the morning was Potkazhan. The houses had slab stone roofs, like those we had seen in Galicia on our first ride through Spain. Laid haphazardly, with tall chimneys poking through, the stones covered low stone houses with few windows. Unusually, the village also had what looked like an English parish church, complete with a tower with a cross on it, and a graveyard with tombstones. Since leaving the Shala Valley, we had seen mosques in most villages. From now on we were to see more evidence of a Christian (Greek Orthodox) past.

As we neared Kalivaç, the last village before the Tahirit Pass, we overtook the local schoolmaster, who was walking along carrying some books and papers. We were just getting through to him our desire to get to Voskopojë by the shortest route, when a brand-new Land Rover Discovery with a Union Jack on the side drove up. It was the first vehicle we had seen in days. Out jumped the local doctor, who spoke excellent English, having once been captain of a ship in which he had sailed to Swansea and Southampton. We had a surreal conversation before he had to rush off, being a busy man. There was time for him to explain our exact needs to everyone, including Durim, who rolled up in the Landcruiser while we were talking. But, before we knew it, a rather startled young man called Tani (Artan Husalari) had agreed, for 4,000 leka, to take us to Lozhan, which lay on the drivable road which lay athwart our route and where we could all meet up again, with any luck. Without further ado, Tani borrowed a horse, a very small bay with spindly legs, which he then rode for nine hours without a saddle or bridle. We soon found ourselves following an obscure track into the hills and my mood lightened.

For the first three hours we followed a tinkling river which ran downhill towards us through a truly delightful gorge. Shepherds and woodsmen were friendly because they knew Tani and he could explain who we were. We realised how the surly lack of eye contact we had so often met came from fear and suspicion of the unknown rather than unfriendliness. Not having to constantly peer into a map, with Tani guiding the way, meant that we could relax and immerse ourselves in the peace and beauty of the landscape we were riding through. We were in deep countryside, far from any road. We plucked plums and blackberries from trees and brambles as we passed and the sun shone warmly on our backs. This gentle landscape soon gave way to a more dramatic and monumental, but no less beautiful, one as we neared the top of the Tahirit Pass (*Gur I Kamjasil*), where we had to nego-tiate some rocky and vertiginous cliff paths until we could gaze down at yet another monumental landscape.

We dropped steeply down to the village of Osnat, which had rather fine houses, some with domed doorways front and back, as we had seen at Arren. There were rich orchards too, where the trees were heavy with red apples and in the muddy, medieval lane past the communal water trough, rosy-cheeked old ladies chatted together and fetching little children played. Two teenage girls sitting on a pile of corn-husks were painting their toenails. They looked up and giggled as we passed. Everyone was welcoming and helpful. For once we could look around, take photographs and make friends, leaving the business of enquiring about the best route ahead to Tani.

From then on, the river we were following flowed with us. It gradually increased in size until it looked as though it would hold fish. Louella saw two turquoise kingfishers flashing past. I began to fantasise about catching supper from a camp beside the river. I was further encouraged when, on joining a road of sorts, we came on several fish farms. One of them had a European flag and a Stars and Stripes, as well as the universal red Albanian flag with its two-headed eagle. We hollered as we rode past, hoping the flags might mean that some friendly foreign aid workers were living there, but they must have been having a siesta, as it was mid-afternoon, and no one appeared. A couple of hours further along and we breasted another ridge, from which our lane zigzagged down to meet a proper dirt road at the bottom of the big valley ahead. This ran from east to west and we hoped our team would be somewhere down there. It looked as though, for once, we would camp before sunset – and I might even have time to fish. For once, too, there was a mobile signal and Tani spoke to Durim on my phone. They had stopped at the village of Lozhan on the far side of the valley. Confidently, Durim told Tani that we should turn right on reaching the valley floor and we would reach them in two kilometres.

We scrambled eagerly downhill, urging our tired horses on. There was a perfect camp site at the bottom. A large river, which looked to my eager eyes to be heaving with fish, ran under a bridge, but our team was not there. They always preferred to camp in a village, although we repeatedly suggested that beside a river would be nice. Feeling a little cross that such a good opportunity had been missed, we hurried on, now urging the poor horses into a canter in our anxiety to arrive in daylight. The road entered a deep, dark gorge and after half an hour or so it became obvious that there were no villages in that direction. Of course there was no signal in the gorge. And so we cantered back again to where there was a signal and discovered that we had been sent the wrong way. We struggled on for another hour to discover that Lozhan, once we found the road there, was high up above the valley and another long climb was asked of our poor horses. The camp site had been set up on a piece of waste ground on a knoll overlooking the valley, where a giant oak tree, the village meeting place, grew. A cold wind blew strongly and although there was no grass, great mounds of hay appeared soon after we arrived. Glasses of raki to toast Tani's excellent navigation and some rousing opera on the car CD soon made us forget the tiring ride. Ylli produced an excellent supper, after which we all went to bed in high spirits, watched by a few drunken villagers who came and went in the firelight.

Tani left before dawn to return to Kalivaç. After the pleasure of having a good guide, I was determined to find another if possible. The road to Voskopojë made another great loop of about 50 km round the mountains, but there was a direct track, once again over a high pass, which we were told could be done in four hours, but would not be easy to find. As we drank our morning coffee, schoolchildren with their satchels came to see us and the horses, and adorably pretty little girls in pink and blue asked if they could have a ride.

One of the noisiest of the previous night's drunks was a toothless old man with a beard and a roguish look. He had returned to the camp and was enjoying a slice of sticky baklava, which Ylli had given him and which was trickling down his beard. We suggested he might like to ride with us to Voskopojë for 3,000 leka and he accepted with alacrity. Mounted sideways on a small grey mare, Nebruz proved a superb guide. Cackling with glee, he led us straight up the mountain behind Lozhan, weaving between the scrubby beech trees as he followed goat tracks, which would have been invisible to us. Once over the top, we scrambled down and up again through an enchanted land of little hidden fields and woods, where water flowed from innumerable springs. These were often led by pipes to drinking places and the horses happily sucked up great draughts. We had an apple each, but with one long upper tooth and two small lower ones, Nebruz found it difficult to eat and had to refuse. He claimed to be forty-three, but looked a great deal older.

As we breasted the next rise and emerged from the trees onto some open ground with a lake in the distance, we heard, to our surprise, the sound of principalities brought prosperity, and by the eighteenth century it was the greatest city in the Balkans, culturally and industrially, larger than Athens or Sofia, with an overall population claimed by some to have been over 60,000 but more realistically around 35,000. As a religious centre, it had seventy churches and the first printing press in the region, which published books in several languages, and a school where some of the finest artists in the region made frescoes and icons. The destruction of the churches began with sacking and pillaging by the Ottomans and culminated in the razing of the city by Vizier Ali Pasha in 1788. Further devastation occurred during the First World War and continued through the Second World War because of all the guerilla activity. Hoxha's atheistic desire to eliminate all traces of religion contributed to the decay, which continued until quite recently through vandalism and bigotry. In 2002, the five churches remaining in Voskopojë were listed among the Top 100 Most Endangered Historical Sites by the World Monuments Fund. Today only one of those churches is used as such, the others being locked up and abandoned or used for agricultural purposes. Voskopojë is now just an inconsequential provincial village; a few hundred farmers eke out a living, carrying hay and leading mules through once grand, now ruined, streets. They are mainly short, dark Vlachs, a pastoral people who are also scattered throughout northern Greece, Romania, Bulgaria and Macedonia.

For me, Voskopojë reflects in microcosm what has happened to Albania as a whole. Once, both were at the very centre of things – busy and dynamic, culturally vibrant, thriving, proud, self-confident, independent and rich – where people of all nations came to trade or paused on their travels across the known world. Then, first under the Romans and successively until the Ottoman Empire, they were almost completely destroyed again and again, until most traces of their former glory have disappeared. There have been many famous and infamous Albanians who have played a significant role in world history. Twenty-six Grand Viziers of the Ottoman Empire are said to have been Albanian. There have been four Albanian Popes, most notably Clement XI (1700–21), Giovanni Francesco Albani, who commissioned during his reign the remarkable 'Illyricum Sacrum', a formidable history, which is today one of the main sources in the field of Albanology. He was a member of the Albani family, which provided the Catholic Church with numerous cardinals and priests. Albanian architects were world renowned and proud patriots claim, sometimes on rather shaky evidence, that they built, among other great edifices, the Blue Mosque in Istanbul in 1562, the incomparable Taj Mahal at Agra for Shah Jahan, completed in 1648, and, of course, all the great Byzantine churches in Voskopojë, which are no more. Aristotle was the son of an Albanian merchant and Al-Albani is considered perhaps the greatest Islamic scholar of the twentieth century. He was born in Shkodra, but lived in Damascus. Mohammed Ali, the founder of the modern Egyptian dynasty which ended with King Farouk, was Albanian, as was Kemal Ataturk, the founder of modern Turkey. Mostly, though, Albanians have been known through the ages for their prowess as politicians and warriors, often combining the two roles. I even came across a suggestion that Napoleon Bonaparte's ancestors migrated from Albania to Corsica as part of the diaspora which began in the fifteenth century with the arrival of the Turks.

David Smiley stayed in a nearby village for some time on his first mission and bought his beloved mule, Fanny, there for five of the gold sovereigns bearing Queen Victoria's head that he and the other British officers who had been dropped into Albania carried in large quantities. Taking inflation into account, it made our horses seem cheap, as sovereigns are worth over £100 today. Smiley writes in his book, *Albanian Assignment*, that over 30,000 sovereigns were dropped to them by the RAF on that mission, which in today's terms is more than £3 million. It was always a worry stopping them falling into the wrong hands. Smiley used to sleep with 4,000 sovereigns buried in the floor under his sleeping bag. Once, a local commissar, to whom he had just paid 200 sovereigns for the hire of mules and mulemen, was found shot dead. It turned out that Smiley's bodyguard had seen him hand the money over and had followed the commissar, killed him and vanished. With that much money he could retire.

Smiley writes that there were still traces of some sixty churches in Voskopojë then, but says many were being looted of their treasures by the Italians. He also told of the custom then prevalent of washing and massaging the feet of arriving guests, a great comfort after walking all day. In Catholic and Greek Orthodox areas, this was done by a girl or woman. In a Muslim house it was usually performed by one of the sons or 'some rugged old warrior servant'. This custom seems to have disappeared – we were never favoured in this way. But other customs Smiley describes – the interminable time it took to prepare an evening meal and the difficulty one had staying awake on glass after glass of raki – were ones we could easily identify with.

We found Mickey sitting at the bar at a crossroads deep in conversation with an attractive Peace Corps girl from Dallas. Jennifer Robertson was exceptionally bright, spoke good Albanian and had been living in Voskopojë for some months. She was doing research on eco-tourism, was extremely well informed about everything and seemed to know everyone. We chatted non-stop with her as we went to see the church of St Nicholas, or *Shenkolle*, where a gentle priest showed us round. The mostly eighteenth-century frescoes inside the church had been badly defaced during the various troubles which had beset Voskopojë over the years. Only a few years ago 'people against everything', as Jennifer described them, had sprayed graffiti and picked out the eyes of saints. Enough was left to give a glimpse of the glory that had once been; some of the frescoes even retained their exquisite colours. In the central aisle, between fine wooden clerical stalls, was an impressive Heath Robinson stove, from which an eccentric chimney duct led across the church to a window, a necessity during the bitterly cold Albanian winters. Five men were working to repair the stone roof, but there is so much more to be done. Voskopojë should be a world heritage site, but most of the buildings we saw were tasteless modern villas and holiday homes being put up without any planning control.

Jennifer found us a guide who was willing to accompany us for two days across country to the town of Frashër. We were just at the point of agreeing a fee of 3,000 leka per day when his wife, carrying a baby and shouting at the top of her voice, ran out of their nearby house. She started to berate her husband, picking up stones and throwing them at him as if he were a donkey, eventually driving him back inside their home. Glowering at us, she stomped

Tracks were marked on the map, but although we searched diligently we could not find them. And so we continued to the west, hoping the track would eventually turn south. It didn't and so very reluctantly we turned back to have another look for a path. There was nothing but scrub and a steep slope, almost a cliff, down which we were reluctant to scramble. We returned to the west, and at last spotted a sheep track. This led down to a green valley where we found a wizened old shepherd carrying a wooden staff and a blue blanket, surrounded by the usual large dogs which, for once, were friendly.

It often seems as though these men have remained undisturbed for centuries – through wars and upheavals, revolutions and occupations, they continue to tread ancient tracks, slowly following their precious flocks, alone in silence save for the bleating and birdsong. We showed him one of our fliers and asked the way to Vithquc. *'Ska problem!'* he said, and walked with us to a forestry track, which led up to the pass ahead. With hand signals and a grin he clearly indicated that we should turn left again there, and in one and a half hours we would be in Vithkuq. Sudden happines replaced the panic and fury at being lost. We felt a surge of affection for all Albanians, with their acceptance of their lot and their humour in the face of adversity. I was reminded that John Belushi, one of the Blues Brothers, was born of parents who came from near there. Perhaps our shepherd, with his laconic smile, was a relation.

When we reached Vithkuq before nightfall we found that our team had set up camp in the middle of the village and Mickey had moved into a hotel next door. We decided to join him, as it was only £5 a night and, although it was basic, there was a little hot water to wash in and we were utterly content; after thrashing about in the undergrowth, we were dirty, sweaty, scratched, sunburnt and covered in dust. There was even a restaurant with fresh trout on which we feasted, giving Durim and Ylli, who joined us, a night off cooking. Smiley describes having 'a giant barbecue' in 1943. 'The Vlachs had roasted sheep whole on spits, and eaten in a pilaf they tasted delicious; there was plenty of raki, chianti, and beer; the celebrations finished with a good deal of singing, and McLean and I joined in an Albanian folk dance. Altogether it was an excellent party, and I strongly suspect that it was all paid for by British sovereigns.'

Louella and Mickey had visited the church, where they were shown round by the priest and three small boys. Louella lit a candle for Merlin in Afghanistan and the priest said a prayer for him. A helpful young schoolmaster called Denis, who spoke some English and was eager to please, was asked to translate the priest's life story and told Mickey and Louella that 'He was born in Vlore and killed in Berat'! The poor priest looked healthy enough and so they assumed he meant 'ordained'. When I joined them, I told him about the problem I was having finding a guide. At that moment, the old man walked past and Denis asked him again if he would take us and he agreed, but only for 10,000. I asked if he had a horse and he said he had a mule. As it was by now 8.30 and the chances of finding anyone else were slim, I reluctantly agreed and he hurried off up the hill to get ready. We were saddled up and on the road an hour later as the already hot sun beat down from a cobalt blue sky, the fourth such day in a row. As we parted to go our separate ways, I asked Durim if there was any chance of rain. 'Impossible!' he replied, and we decided not to weigh ourselves down with wet weather gear.

To reach our guide, Nico's, house we had to climb up a very steep cobbled lane between some houses. The transformation was dramatic. The sleazy boozer had changed into an apple-cheeked farmer clad in tweed jacket and sensible shoes. His buxom wife and a grandson walked with us until we were out of the village. His mule was strong and we made good time, climbing over passes and weaving around through short cuts that we would never have found by ourselves. We saw almost no one except a couple of woodsmen and once we reached the logging roads the going became easier. We came to an isolated village called Selenica in a little over two hours. Nico stopped to ask for directions and a heated discussion evolved into a shouting match with the ladies of the village, who were eager to help, but were not telling him what he wanted to hear. '*Ska rruga!*' they kept saying, 'No road'. Nico was becoming more and more irate and it puzzled me, too. How could there be no road; and why would someone who had lived in the neighbouring village for seventy years need to ask for directions? But these villages are singular in their remoteness.

In my experience throughout the world, any two or three neighbouring villages will have good lines of communication between them, but not in Albania. After yet more shouting and gesticulating, Nico decided to follow their directions, and we made a wide loop through the woods. Once in the open again, we came upon a formidable shepherdess carrying a big stick and wearing Wellington boots, a thick woollen cardigan and a cloth cap. She had a large flock and some savage dogs, which she made no effort to call off. They attacked Bora, who was brave and kicked out at them with her hind legs and then reared up to do the same with her front feet. Nico and the shepherdess screamed at each other but not about the dogs – I realised that they were actually exchanging directions.

The village of Clirim, which we reached in the early afternoon, looked about half way to Frashër on the map. It was a scruffy place, but it had a bar and we thought it would be nice to stop for a cold drink. As we were unsaddling, a bossy, official-looking man approached and insisted we walk with him straight on out of town. We followed, looking back nostalgically as our only chance to eat and drink anything other than water from road-side springs faded into the distance.

Nico, on his mule, Ruska, could keep up a faster pace than us for much of the time, especially over rough ground. Sitting sideways, with his legs stuck out jiggling constantly, he thrummed the mule's sides with his heels, while beating it gently but repeatedly with a stick. With his other hand, he held bunches of leafy beech twigs, with which he fed her. In this way he was able to keep up an almost constant trot. Our horses tended to plod and needed ceaseless urging. Although they were amazingly stoical and brave when we led them over difficult terrain, they trod carefully and often stopped, jerking our arms as we led them. In many ways, we agreed, mules are a better form of transport, and we have ridden them from time to time, but we couldn't quite see ourselves making a long journey on them. David Smiley describes crossing a range of mountains not far to the west of where we were. The partisans had given him an ex-Italian army horse to ride.

My horse was very unsure of itself on the mountain tracks, continually slipping and stumbling, until finally it slipped and fell over the edge of the track. I was riding at the time, but managed to slip my feet out of the stirrups and throw myself off as the unfortunate animal fell over a sheer drop of over a hundred feet and was killed. I determined never to ride a horse in the mountains again, for the mules were uncannily surefooted, and Fanny never gave me a fall in all the months I rode her.

If I had read that before we left, I might well have decided to take mules instead, and I realise how lucky we were to take our brave horses along so many dangerous cliffs without mishap.

The official took us to the top of a hill beyond Clirim and spent a long time pointing out a direct route across the deep canyon ahead, which would save us having to follow the road all the way around the outside of the mountain. I was becoming suspicious of short cuts, which often took longer and exhausted the horses more than staying on the road; but I was overruled. It was a steep and difficult descent which we half walked, half scrambled down only to get lost at the bottom. We needed my compass to find our way back to the road, which at that point crossed a substantial river by a fine old Ottoman bridge, one section of which had been destroyed and replaced with a crude Bailey bridge. This consisted of rotten planks, many of which were missing or had holes in them. There was no way we could take animals across. Nico led his mule down to the boulder-strewn river bed and we had to go some way along the bank before we found a place to cross.

Bora preferred to make her own way, rather than to be led. As a result, Louella often let her have her head, either following at her own pace or hanging on to her tail when going up steep slopes. Now Bora thought she would cross the river on her own, and did so. This left Louella stranded, as she would have had to swim to get across. Fortunately, Bora was obedient as well as intelligent and independent, and she crossed back when called so that Louella could ride over.

leaving a network of faint trails through the woods. A slight deviation would have taken us miles in the wrong direction and spelled disaster, since there were many deep parallel valleys, and I had to concentrate hard with compass and map to make sure we were on the right contour. The going now was not only good underfoot – an earthy path shaded by attractive, mature groves of beech – but we had uninterrupted views from the ridge of serried, forested hills. Time slowed, afternoon advanced towards evening and clouds gathered. Suddenly, it started to rain. We sheltered under an overhanging tree and emerged fairly dry when the storm had passed. On again and then, just as we reached the very highest point and were hoping that we would soon be going downhill, the heavens opened and a proper storm broke. We tried to shelter but were soon soaked and we had not a shred of waterproof covering between us, only our fleeces, in which we wrapped our cameras. Blinding flashes of lightning were followed instantly by deafening crashes of thunder as the storm swirled close around us. We were right in the centre of the thunderstorm and, with all the metal on our saddles, bridles, cameras and mobiles, it seemed quite possible that we would attract a bolt of lightning. The horses were surprisingly calm and just turned their rumps into the driving rain and hung their heads. After twenty minutes with no let up, we decided we could get no wetter and rode on into the downpour.

As suddenly as it had started, the rain stopped, the sun came out and we began to steam. Even better, as the clouds dispersed we could see our way ahead and a distinct path meandering down to Frashër. It proved to be no more than a goat track in parts and quite impossible for any vehicle. When it crossed screes where the chalky, limestone hillside had collapsed in landslides, I found myself once again riding with my eyes shut as brave Semi picked his way along a foot-wide ledge above a plummeting drop. The views were outstanding, but I didn't dare look at them much and we were all by now only interested in getting to our camp. After nine hours in the saddle, we finally did, something the locals in Frashër seemed to think a record time. 'Should have taken at least twelve to fifteen,' they muttered, as though we had somehow cheated fate by arriving while it was still daylight.

We drank glasses of raki to get the warmth back into our bones and made a great fuss of Nico. He had wanted to turn back for home once Frashër came in sight, but we persuaded him to spend the night with us. I lent him a towel and old tracksuit of mine, since his clothes were soaked, and we all had a very jolly dinner of Ylli's best hot soup and rice while listening to the strains of Pavarotti.

Frashër is the birthplace of the Frashëri brothers – Abdyl, Naim and Sami – who played a major part in Albania's history. Abdyl, the eldest, made a speech at a town called Prizren in 1878 and it was this that stoked the first flames of Albanian nationalism. The first proper Albanian political organisation, the Prizren League, was formed, which sought autonomy under the Ottoman Empire and would eventually lead to Albanian independence. Much of the initial impetus for the movement came from a frustrated desire for Albanians to be allowed to speak their own tongue. Albanian is a very old Indo-European language with a rich oral tradition. Derived from Illyrian, it stands alone as the only example of a linguistic group going back to at least the seventh century BC and so is one of Europe's oldest languages. Although it survived the centuries of Roman rule, unlike Greek it was not written down and did not have a coherent alphabet until 1908, after what became known as the 'Battle of the Alphabets'. The Catholics in the north had used the Latin alphabet, the Orthodox in the south used the Greek and some Albanian Muslims used Arabic characters. Today the Albanian alphabet has thirty-six letters, some of which have no exact equivalent in English.

All three Frashëri brothers spent much of their lives in Istanbul campaigning in their different ways. Abdyl, the politician, went to prison and died young as a result. Naim, the second son, became one of Albania's greatest poets, writing passionate nationalistic 'paeans of homesickness' with titles like *Wolf and Lamb*, *Livestock and Agriculture* and *The Bird and the Boy*. They were written in simple Albanian so that uneducated people could read them, and were smuggled into the country packed in sacks of grain. To be caught reading anything in Albanian was to be punished severely by the Turkish authorities.

Sami, the youngest, was fluent in nine languages and it was he who drew up the phonetic alphabet that is used today. At first, its purpose was to spread knowledge of reading and writing in Albanian and it was secretly intro- duced into all sorts of schools, even an American Protestant one. Sami used this as a propaganda tool through the newspaper he edited in Istanbul. He wrote: 'Why are Albanians deprived of a right which every nation on earth has? Not to be able to write and learn their own language . . . ' Although, largely through the efforts of the Frashëri brothers, Albania declared itself independent of the Ottoman Empire in 1912, it was not recognised as an independent sovereign state by Europe and admitted to the League of Nations until 1921.

The Frashëri brothers were members of the Bektashi sect, as were many of Albania's revolutionaries, like Skanderbeg and Ali Pasha, through the ages. Bektashism, a Sufi order, is part of the Islamic mystic tradition. It was founded in Turkey in the thirteenth century by a Persian mystic, Haji Bektash Veli. It spread to the Balkans and became particularly strong in Albania. One reason for this, I was told, was that so many Christian boys were taken forcibly from there to serve as janissaries in the Ottoman army. Forced to convert to the Bektashi form of Islam, they were highly trained and became the elite forces, disciplined and celibate, so that they were the scourge of Europe. In time they grew to be rich and very powerful as kingmakers, rather like the Knights Templar, and in due course they, too, were massa- cred in 1826 by Sultan Mahmud II, who had 60,000 killed on one occasion in Istanbul. In 1925, Kemal Atatürk, whose father was an Albanian from Kosovo, banned all Sufi orders and the Bektashi headquarters, which had always been in Turkey, was relocated to Tirana. In Turkey, rather than attaching blame to Atatürk for this action, Turkish Bektashis supported him both financially and in terms of their very great influence, as the reforms largely were those long desired by the third of Turks who were of the Bektashi and associated Alevi movement.

Like all religious communities in Albania, the Bektashi suffered terribly under the communist regime between 1945 and 1990. Many *babas* and dervishes were executed or sent to hard labour camps, as were the representatives of all religions, which were outlawed in what was to become the world's first atheist state. Their land and properties were expropriated and their *tekkes*, or meeting places, were destroyed. Following the collapse of communism, the Bektashi community has re-emerged; it now operates in thirty-one countries and numbers over 200 million adherents.

On my recce, while I was in Tirana, Auron had taken me to meet the *dedebaba* or head of the order, Hadji Dede Reshat Bardhi, and I had been mightily impressed. As soon as I went into the reception room to sit and talk with another of the *babas* until the great man arrived, I felt completely at home. There were paintings of saints and animals on the walls. The iconography was surprisingly familiar. One of the saints, who was riding on a lion, could have been St Jerome; another was riding on a white horse and holding a baby; and there were terracotta figures which could have been groups of Christian saints. I asked how this could be, as I understood Islam prohibited the representation of people and animals. 'The prophet said that in his time he should not be the subject of idolatry. We respect our saints, but we do not pray to them. These are like family photographs,' said the *baba*. The man on the lion was a saint who had got rid of all his sins, which were represented by the animals around: the lion, wolves, deer and rams. In this way he achieved perfection. But the man next to him did so by making rocks fly and this was cleverer than taming animals. Also, it showed humility, which is important. The man on the horse was one of the Twelve Imams, who are like our twelve apostles, with the one big difference – they came one after the other, not altogether.

The *baba* who told me all this was a large man with a full grey beard and exuded jollity. He had served in the army with Auron and, as is the tradition with Bektashism, had foregone worldly things. Known for their liberal views and their non-conformity – they do not fast during Ramadan, they drink in moderation and they do not normally attend mosques – Bektashis are also famed for their wit. There are many Bektashi jokes which mock the solemnity of orthodox mullahs, but the sincerity of their own belief shines through. One example: due to the pressure of friends, a Bektashi went with them to a Mosque at Friday noon. During the sermon the imam was describing in vivid detail all of the natural and religious reasons why drinking alcohol is bad. As an illustration, the imam said, 'If you put a bucket of water and a bucket of wine in front of a donkey, which one will it drink? The water, of course. Now why would a donkey choose to drink the water and not the wine?' Unable to control himself, the Bektashi shouted out, 'Because it's a donkey, that's why!'

When the *dedebaba* himself arrived, he kissed me on both cheeks, his big white beard softly brushing against them. An imposing figure, he exuded an aura of sanctity. I said how happy I was to be learning about Bektashism, which is not well known in England, and that it was such a contrast to the false image of Islam which terrorism had brought about. I asked him how he thought we should fight it. He replied that Bektashis follow the true teaching of Mohammed. When you join you start a new life. Knowledge is what matters, not numbers but quality. To combat terrorism, he said, first you must cut off their finance; then bring Bektashis to the West to show the true Islam.

His green and white robes were splendid and topped by a green and white round hat. He had a large red signet ring mounted in silver on his wedding ring finger and another silver ring on the same finger of his other hand. He said, 'Knowledge is power and religion is knowledge. The prophet says you should respect people of other religions. They too believe in God. It is not their fault they are not Muslims.' I said, 'The greatest strength is to pity your enemy'. He nodded and replied, 'Judge people not from your point of view but from their own.' I told him I was writing a book about Albania and described the journey we were planning. 'When you ride around this country on a horse you will start to learn more about Albania,' he said. 'Three things will accompany you to your grave: your children; your possessions; and your knowledge. The first two will return home; only the third will stay with you. If you have written a book you will be remembered. If you don't write, then it is forgotten.'

I asked about how one became a Bektashi *baba*. 'You choose. No one forces you. For seven years you are a servant and you are told all the time "Do not join!" If you pass the tests, and there are many tests, you become a dervish. [Not a whirling dervish – those are of the Mevlevi Order.] After another seven years, you may become a *baba*, a saint. There is only one *dedebaba*, who is called the grandfather of all Bektashis and no one has the right to challenge his authority.'

Today about a quarter of all Albanians would say they are Bektashi and the order plays a powerful role behind the scenes in Albanian affairs. Their liberal and humanistic views contrast strongly with the rigidity of the orthodox Islamic and Christian views with which we are all too familiar. They see the good in all creeds, maintaining that man is the highest expression of divine power and that he creates heaven or hell for himself by his own actions. They preach tolerance, charity to all men, respect for women, humility, industry and the rejection of violence. I found my meeting with their leader inspiring and I came away wishing that this could be the face of religion in the modern world. Later, the *baba* took me round the impressive building works of the new Bektashi meeting place, a fine domed edifice which will tower over Tirana once it is completed. It is being financed mainly by the prosperous Bektashi communities in the USA and will make a suitable head-quarters for the sect.

We had camped next to the Frashëri brothers' house, now a museum, which we were allowed to look round. It was the first building we had been in on our rural route which felt like a real country house. A substantial building, it had a fine roof made of flat stone, but the windows were small and there were no concessions to comfort. There was a metal plaque on the front and three large busts of the brothers, all bearded, moustachioed and with a strong resemblance to each other. Inside, the rooms were mostly empty, with only a few photographs and mementos to indicate that it was a museum. In one room there were comfortable mattresses and sheepskins which we were told we were welcome to sleep on. Louella was keen to do so, Mickey said he was afraid of ghosts, Ylli and I thought we should stay near the horses and Durim wouldn't stay there alone, so we all slept at the camp.

Reaching Frashër was a significant moment for us. It meant that we had made our way through the hard interior of the country, following routes barely visited by outsiders since the war, and were now on the threshold of entering the part of Albania made forever famous by Byron. From now on the character both of the landscape and our journey would change. There was now no doubt that we would complete what we had set out to do and we could allow ourselves a moment to savour the sweet smell of success. As I lay and gazed up at an exact half moon, replete with too much raki and washed over by the strains of *The Magic Flute* coming from the Landcruiser's stereo, I felt able to relax for the first time for days.

PART IV

Byron Country

Chapter 14

Childe Harold Rode Here

What rainbow tints, what magic charms are found.
Rock, river, forest, mountain all abound,
And bluest skies that harmonise the whole.
Byron, *Childe Harold's Pilgrimage*

Byron was the *enfant terrible* of London society at the beginning of the eighteenth century. In spite of being born with a club foot, his good looks, curly dark hair and powerful blue eyes made him irresistible to both sexes. When, in 1809, debts and scandal made a departure for Europe imperative, he borrowed £4,800 and set out with his friend John Hobhouse and his faithful valet, William Fletcher. The Napoleonic Wars made a conventional Grand Tour of France, Italy and Germany impossible, and so they went to Portugal, Spain, Albania, Greece and Turkey instead. During this time, Byron wrote his epic semi-autobiographical poem, *Childe Harold's Pilgrimage*, which was to be such a success when published on his return to England. Of all the literary threads we were pursuing, this was undoubtedly the most fun.

The three Englishmen rode up from Iannina, in what is Greece today, and reached Tepelenë in seven days. Byron was captivated by Albania's wild and rugged landscape. He describes mountains covered in thick forests as far as the eye could reach, great chasms, jagged ranges and madly dashing rivers. It was here that his love of Nature in her richest majesty was fulfilled and his poetry took on a greater intensity.

It rained heavily in the night, water dripped onto our sleeping bags and a big bulge grew above our heads, as a fold in our tent filled up. We had to wait until the sun rose to dry off our clothes. There was one spot where we could receive a signal on our mobiles and, having been out of contact for a while, there were several messages. Auron Tare was due to join us and he was arranging for some journalists and Albanian television crews to interview us. Crown Prince Leka also rang to say he planned to drive down and see us. We thought the story of how we had met at Sandhurst and how his friend Merlin was now in Afghanistan might interest the media. General Luan Hoxha, the Albanian Chief of Defence, who I had met on my recce, told me he was proud of the fact that thirty Albanian soldiers were fighting in Afghanistan alongside our son.

After we left Frashër our route was to be straightforward and therefore there was no need of a guide. A long and very winding dirt road led at first over a pass and then down to the Vjosë River far below. We followed the river into a little-visited national park, the Fir of Hotova, named after the silver fir that grows abundantly in the region. In this pristine wilderness of mature forests and deep valleys, wildlife thrives. Even though we only saw jays and flocks of crows, brown bears, wolves, foxes, martens, deer and wild boar are said to be common. The silence was absolute, disturbed by only two lorries in the next five hours, and the uninterrupted forest that spread in all directions was truly stupendous. We eventually emerged from the cool shade of the woods to look out over a great open space that led the eye towards a wall of barren mountains that lay between us and the Adriatic coast. It was into these mountains that Bill Tilman, the oldest SOE officer to operate in Albania, was dropped. At forty-five, Tilman was already a legend as one of Britain's greatest mountaineers. He had attempted to climb Everest three times and was the leader of the 1938 expedition, climbing without oxygen to over 27,000 feet. He was also a hero of the First World War, having been awarded two Military Crosses while still in his teens and been wounded three times. He said he was looking forward to his time in Albania, 'as there were so many mountains to climb'. He soon forged himself a formidable reputation by scaling a peak every morning before breakfast, outdoing even the toughest local mountain men, and by bathing daily outside in a freezing spring. In 1977, at the age of seventy-nine, he set out with a very young team – all in their twenties – to sail to Smith Island in the Antarctic in order to attempt the first ascent of Mount Foster. Their boat and the entire crew disappeared in the South Atlantic. Mount Foster remained unclimbed for another twenty years and no trace of Tilman or his team has ever been found.

As we gazed over the fine view and wondered whether we would be able to see the sea, we came upon a neat new building, the Park's headquarters. Nearby, spanning the road, was an impressive arched gateway made of logs to mark the entrance. A little gully beside the road was piled full of plastic litter and other rubbish. It would have been hard to demonstrate more clearly the contrast between Albania's natural beauty and the disastrous impact of man upon it.

It would be easy to believe that the abundance of litter is a symptom of ignorance, poverty and lack of facilities, but this would be wrong. Under communism, glass and paper were scrupulously recycled and schoolchildren were indoctrinated in the importance of saving waste and keeping their country clean. It has been suggested that the excessive and profligate scattering of rubbish everywhere today may actually be a subconscious reaction against those restrictive days and a way of celebrating the free availability of consumer goods.

We intended to attempt a crossing of the wide, swirling waters of the Vjosë by a suspension bridge I had found on my recce and then to follow the far bank to a rendezvous at the next bridge with our crew, thus avoiding staying on a dangerous main road. Straight out of an Indiana Jones movie, the bridge looked on the verge of collapse. Several planks were missing, revealing vertigo-inducing drops to the torrent below, and everything swayed alarmingly as we led the horses over. Balancing ourselves with arms outstretched and, for me at least, eyes half shut, we looked rather foolish next to our brave horses who didn't turn a hair as they crossed.

The faint path on the far bank was interrupted frequently by deep, over-grown gullies which ran right down to the river. Negotiating these involved a lot of scrambling and backtracking, so that some 10 km took us two and a half hours. As we passed the town of Këlcyrë, the mountains of Hormovë and Trebeshinë on either side closed in on us. Through the narrow canyon courses the River Vjosë, which is too deep to cross with horses. Many great battles have taken place here over the ages as the defile, which used to be called the *Fauces Antigonenses*, has been the key to control of southern Albania and Epirus ever since Roman times and probably for long before.

In 198 BC this gorge was held by Philip V, King of Macedon, as he confronted a punitive expedition sent from Rome under the command of the Consul Flaminius. The Romans had recently defeated Hannibal and were now bent on consolidating their power throughout Greece and the Balkans. The armies faced each other through the gorge, about 8 km apart, but with Philip in an impregnable position. The gorge is so narrow and has such high sides that almost no army, even one representing the might of Rome, could break through a well-defended position. A shepherd came to Flaminius and said he knew of a track that led over Mount Trebeshinë, which towers above the gorge. Four thousand footsoldiers and 3,000 horsemen crept along this perilous route through the night with muffled armour. The remaining Roman army made feints to distract the Macedonians and to draw them deep into the gorge. At a prearranged smoke signal, which indicated that the 7,000 Romans had managed to get behind the Macedonian army, those left in the gorge attacked. The Macedonians were driven back only to find another Roman force behind them. They were routed, broke and fled. It was the beginning of the end of the empire Alexander the Great had created little over a hundred years before. Within a year imperial power had passed from his successor to Rome and Macedon was never to pose a threat again.

Early in the Second World War, Mussolini made the disastrous decision to invade Greece without proper preparation. In January 1941, one of his crack regiments, the 77th Infantry, belonging to the Lupi di Toscana (The

Wolves of Tuscany), was annihilated in the Gorge of Këlcyrë, with 300 prisoners being taken.

By July 1944 the Germans were in retreat. They were being attacked by British Commandos on the coast, and inland they were being harried by the communist partisans, who were by then dominant in the south of the country. Like a scorpion surrounded by fire, their reprisals became more atrocious. In one clash that month, a group of local patriots ambushed a German patrol in the Këlcyrë Gorge and killed two soldiers. All the men of the town abandoned Këlcyrë and fled up into the mountains, leaving the women and children behind in the belief that they would not be harmed. The Germans closed off the town and forbade anyone to leave. They then set fire to it and 250 women and children were burned to death.

As we rode into the gorge, we could see the dramatic ruins of an ancient fort built by the local ruling family to guard the passage below Mount Trebeshinë. In the late nineteenth century the then Bey of Këlcyrë, Xhemal, was shot from the opposite mountain, Hormovë, while drinking coffee on his terrace – something he did every day. As a result of a long dispute over the grazing on that side of the gorge, the villagers had decided to kill him, but he was well protected by many bodyguards. Three men volunteered to take the extremely long shot across the valley, and one succeeded.

This was the route by which we were now approaching Tepelenë from the north-east. Edward Lear came in from the north on 31 October 1858, through another gorge below the confluence of the Vjosë and the Drini:

> The pure, cloudless sky is of the palest amber hue over the eastern mountains, whose outlines are dimmed by a few filmy vapours; and all is still except the formidable Viósa [sic] murmuring in its white stony channel. It was too chill to ride, even had the mule-tracks – rudely-marked ledges or broken paths by the side of precipices – tempted me to do so. The route ascends the Viósa to the dark gorge, which is so narrow as to allow only the passage of the river, and when that is swollen, it must close this communication

altogether . . . where the cliffs rise perpendicularly to a great height above the stream, or where the path mounts by corkscrew ascent over the rocks, and the eye looks down on the abyss below, the effect is very imposing. The whole morning passed in threading the winding vale of the Viósa, through scenes of wild grandeur, but possessing no particular quality of novelty or beauty. The mountain of Khórmovo [sic], ever in view, gave the chief character to the walk, delightful as it was from the exquisite autumnal weather . . .

It was nearly three P.M. ere the last tedious windings of the valley disclosed the great mountain Trebushin [sic], and its neighbour Khórmovo visible now from base to summit – each calmly towering in bright purple below peaks of glittering snow. Beneath them the junction of the two rivers Viósa and Bantja forms the long promontory of Tepeléni [sic], whose ruined palace and walls and silver-toned mosque give a strange air of dreamy romance to this scene, one of the most sublime and simple in Albania, and certainly one most fraught with associations ancient and modern.

My curiosity had been raised to its very utmost to see this place, for so many years full of the records of one of the most remarkable of men; yet it seemed so strange, after all one had read of the 'no common pomp' of the entertainer of Lord Byron and Sir J.C. Hobhouse, to find a dreary, blank scene of desolation, where once, and so recently, was all the rude magnificence of Oriental despotism!

Byron and Hobhouse arrived from the south. Here is Hobhouse's description:

. . . we crossed the bridge [over the river Drino], which was of stone, but narrow, and of a bad construction, being so high in the middle, as to render it adviseable to dismount in passing over it. Immediately after getting across, we went along a path on the ledge of a steep precipice, with the river, which was broad (perhaps seventy feet), deep, and very rapid, rolling underneath. As we advanced on this bank of the river, we saw the hills to the east spotted with flocks of sheep and goats, and having a line of villages as far as the eye could reach.

In two hours from the bridge, the river began to widen considerably, and a little way further it was augmented by a stream of some breadth [the Vjosë], flowing out of a narrow valley from the north-east. Not long after the junction of the rivers, the whole stream appeared as broad as the Thames at Westminster Bridge, but looking shallower in many places, with gravel banks above the water. Soon afterwards we had a view of Tepellenè [sic], the termination of our journey, which we saw situated immediately on the bank of the river, and, in three quarters of an hour, we entered the native place of Ali.

Tepelenë is so hemmed in by mountains that these are effectively the only three ways it can be approached. All three journeys – Byron's, Lear's and ours – would converge at that point.

But first we had to make our own way through the gorge, and that was not to prove nearly as easy as we had expected. Soon after we had passed the fort, at one of the most inaccessible parts of the river bank, where no one could get except on foot or, with some difficulty, by horse, we came on a little white-painted church. It had a small apse with a cross on top and everything was freshly painted and obviously cherished. There was not another person or building anywhere near and the door was locked. Eventually, we found our team waiting by an attractive hotel and restaurant among some trees by the next bridge and agreed that we would all eat there that night. We were shown two basic rooms and, as he always needed to use every hour of available electricity, it was decided that Mickey should stay in one and we would use the other. As it turned out, we would have been more comfortable camping with the others across the river, as our bed was propped up on bits of plastic plumbing and missing several slats so that it sagged deeply in the middle. We ended up trying to sleep across it and rotating in a full circle like the hands of a clock, trying to get comfortable.

Dinner was goat, which I enthused about, as one so seldom finds it in England and it can be delicious. Unfortunately, this one was old and very chewy, but Auron Tare joined us and the conversation flowed. He was pleased that we were at last joining the Byron Trail, the route followed by Byron and Hobhouse in October 1809, which he wants to develop one day as a tourist route. Auron, who is very knowledgeable and opinionated, tends to take over peoples' lives and we made great plans for the next few days for filming and interviews with the press. After organising everything for the last weeks, it was a great relief to be with someone so full of ideas. He chose to sleep out in the open in his sleeping bag, as he was to do every night that he camped with us from then on. Ylli, who worked for Auron, and Durim, who knew him well, were noticeably more cheerful now the real boss had arrived. I was happy to hand over this role and when it came to discussing our route the next day, I found myself up against articulate and forceful advice, with which it was hard to argue. I wanted to ride the next seven-odd kilometres along the main road to the next bridge heading west until we were within sight of Tepelenë, where we would rendezvous with Auron and receive directions on how to join Byron's route back to the south-east. Durim and Ylli were dead against this idea from the moment I suggested it. I wondered if this could be because they knew I would insist on them driving slowly behind us and I knew how much they hated that. Ylli, who was born in a village nearby, insisted that it would be much quicker and easier to continue along the far side of the river to the road and that there was a good track. Reluctantly, I took this advice but we were soon to regret it. The next morning we found that there was no track; it ended by taking us four hours to do what would have taken one by road at a steady trot, and we hit some of the most difficult terrain for horses that we had met the whole way through the country. A tiny path along dangerous scree led us through a series of tricky gullies until we came to a major tributary of the Vjosë, a river called Zagorisë. Ahead of us lay a wide estuary which we had to cross, but with no visible way out on the far side.

Here we entered a fine stand of maple trees, the oldest and best we had seen so far, and stopped to rest in the shade under them. Balkan maple (*Acer pseudoplatanus*) is what we call sycamore and it is native to Central Europe.

Before we left England, a friend of ours had been told a story by one of the world's leading violin makers, or *lutiers*. He had told him that all the finest violins have always been made from maple wood from Albania and that they still are. This trade, organised by Bulgarian gypsies, is centuries-old and the wood is highly prized by *lutiers* the world over. There, supposedly, is not one Stradivari, Amati or Guarneri violin or cello that has not been made with Albanian maple. Even today, the gypsies still deliver this 'toneful' green wood, which is harvested in a sustainable, ecological way and transported from its source in carts, to violin workshops around the world. Many of the finished musical instruments are then shipped to China for final varnishing. I told this story to many Albanian experts and none had heard about the Bulgarian gypsy connection. It all seems most unlikely and perhaps it is a secret trade which happens clandestinely, but I was assured that the story is true. I later learned that much of the wood used today for violin making comes from sycamore from the north of England.

There are no longer as many trees in Albania as there once were. We know that Hoxha had many forests razed in order to stop the invaders of his paranoid imagination from parachuting into them and hiding. Edward Lear, writing in 1848, certainly found more trees here than in the rest of the Balkans:

> . . . you have there which is found neither in Greece nor in Italy, a profusion everywhere of the most magnificent foliage recalling the greenness of our own island – clustering plane and chestnut, growth abundant of forest oak and beech, and dark tracts of pine.

And, of course, it was not just the forests that were finer then.

> You have majestic cliff-girt shores; castle-crowned heights, and gloomy fortresses; palaces glittering with gilding and paint; mountain passes such as you encounter in the snowy regions of Switzerland; deep bays and blue seas with bright, calm isles resting on the horizon; meadows and grassy knolls;

convents and villages; olive-clothed slopes and snow-capped mountain peaks – and with all this a crowded variety of costume and pictorial incident such as bewilders and delights an artist at each step he takes.

Having crossed the boulder-strewn river bed, which was not kind on the horses' feet, and forded the river, we tried to continue along the bank of the Vjosë. Here the river was overhung by a cliff, but we could see a track high up, which seemed to run round the corner. With the greatest difficulty, we dragged our horses up, only to find that it was a water course. We followed it for a time, although it was narrow and overgrown, only for it to become a metal pipe anchored to the cliff edge. Turning back and persuading the horses to drop down the cliff was even more difficult than getting them up. Not far from us, across the deep Vjosë, ran the level and easy main road.

It took us a long time to find a track out of the bed of the Zagorisë and up to the village of Peshtan. It was a pretty place but we hurried through it crossly and found the road back down to the Vjosë. There we found a new bridge, not marked on my map, which we crossed and then trotted to the rendezvous. It was now midday and we and the horses were exhausted. Ylli seemed genuinely quite unaware of his error in persuading us not to take the road. Looking at the map carefully after the event, we could see that there were at least two preferable routes to the one we had been sent on. After some more road work, we cut back into the hills, climbing steeply, at first on a dirt road then on over a series of tough, stony passes following a difficult goat track, where the horses had to step over and between dangerous boulders. We managed to get lost again but were kindly shown the way, after a substantial detour, by a friendly man on a mule who had been collecting berries with his wife. He rode the mule, of course, and she walked behind carrying the berries.

Now, at last, we were on the Byron Trail proper. Looking back down the wide valley we had entered, we could see where the Vjosë River, debouching from the Gorge of Këlcyrë, was joined by the Drino, running up from inside Greece. In the distance was the town of Tepelenë, crowned with the walls of Ali Pasha's fortress. Born in 1744, Ali Pasha's surname was Arslan, the

Turkish word for lion. Known as the 'Lion of Janina', after the Greek town which was his capital, he was to become the epitome of a cruel and blood-thirsty tyrant, beheading, impaling and roasting his enemies until he was feared throughout the Balkans. He intrigued with Napoleon, who twice offered to make him king of the region, but he preferred the British, so Byron and Hobhouse, when they visited him in 1809 on their way to Greece, were well received by him, Byron with especial enthusiasm, as we shall see.

We passed through Lekël, a charming little place topped with a new church and cloister, in which three donkeys were sheltering from the heat of the sun. Two old ladies indicated that they had heard of Hormovë, which lay next on our route, but they had no idea how to get there.

Hormovë, which Hobhouse calls Korvë and Lear Khórmovo, was destroyed by Ali Pasha and all its inhabitants slaughtered because of an incident that had occurred when he was a child. His mother and his sister were kidnapped and held there for a time. Ali Pasha never forgot and, once he was powerful enough, he had his revenge. It was also the site of another appalling act of German reprisal for guerilla activity in 1944, when thirty-five men of the village were arbitrarily shot because guerillas had been active in the area. Hobhouse writes that it was, in his day, 'more romantically situated than the others . . . crowned with a dome and minaret rising from amidst a grove of cypresses'. He also describes the hills around as being covered with trees, but all is very different now: there are just bare scrubby hillsides and the mosque is no more, presumably destroyed during one of Hoxha's athiest purges. There was an excellent water trough, which cooled us all down. The narrow lanes between the cluster of houses had delicious figs and grapes hanging over the walls, which we were able to pluck and eat from our horses without breaking step. We shared this bounty with them, reaching forward to put whole bunches of grapes in their mouths. Since these villages, too, were largely depopulated, many of the fruit crops just go to waste and no one ever objected to us helping ourselves. In fact they urged us on.

Leaving Hormovë, we followed an ancient trail which ran high on the mountainside and must once have been safer than the bandit-ridden lowlands.

In the Middle Ages there was a well-paved road here for horses and mules and from time to time we could see traces of it, but most of it had completely vanished and the tracks meandered over the hillside, in and out of the many ravines, requiring considerable agility.

We had hoped to reach Labovë, where Byron and Hobhouse stayed on their way both to and from Tepelenë, but we were running late. After a while, we could see the village of Terbuq ahead and I called Auron to say we should all meet there instead. It looked to be about an hour's ride away. Once again I was mistaken as a deep canyon, invisible from where we were, cut across our route and there seemed no way across. Flood water had eroded the sandy sides and turned them into steep-sided cliffs with just a few precipitous goat tracks on which to ascend them. We tried going straight ahead and I found a place that I thought we just might be able to persuade the horses to scramble up. I climbed up to the top and saw a shepherd grazing his flock some distance away. I shouted 'Labovë!' to him and he firmly gestured that we would have to go all the way up the mountain to where the canyon began. However, our horses were immensely agile and we managed to get across not far above this point, where I could just climb up myself. Semi followed without my telling him to and Louella let Bora run free so she found her own way up by a different route. After half an hour of pushing through thick undergrowth spiked with thorns that tore our clothes and shredded our skin we finally reached Terbuq.

An old man sat very still under a huge old oak tree on the village green, watching us. As our eyes locked, there was a distinct frisson and he held my gaze as we rode up to him. *'Mirë dita,'* I said in my best Albanian, *'Me vienkeq. Un nuk de Shqip,'* and I gave him a flier, which he scrutinised, then welcomed us formally to his village. Later, he told Auron that he was remembering the days under communism, when troublemakers rode horses into town. 'But they never came in daylight!'

A small boy, who spoke some words of English well, led us to the water trough so that our horses could drink and soon after everyone arrived and we set up camp under an ancient maple, its leaves beginning to turn amber and russet at the onset of autumn. We pegged out the horses and the old man appeared, staggering under armfuls of sweet hay for them. He had also brought us great bunches of succulent black grapes – *'Americano!'* he called them, with a big grin – and a herb, *çaj mali* (*Alchemilla Vulgaris* or Lady's Mantle), to make tea with. Ylli brewed some up, which we drank and found interesting, if rather bitter.

Auron arrived with film crews from two of Albania's main TV channels, as well as the BBC correspondent from Tirana. As we prepared for the evening, they filmed and interviewed us. The first question is always, 'What is your impression of Albania?' And to this we always replied, without hesitation, that the scenery was the most beautiful in Europe and the people the most hospitable. This went down well and we meant it. Byron recognised the Albanians' instinctive hospitality and kindness and contrasted it with the absence of these qualities in more 'civilised' societies. In *Childe Harold* he tells of his surprise at the 'welcome hand' extended to his party when they first stepped ashore. They

> Led them o'er rocks and past the dangerous swamp,
> Kinder than Polished slaves though not so bland,
> And piled the hearth, and wrung their garments damp,
> And spread their fare; though homely, all they had:
> Such conduct bears Philanthropy's rare stamp:
> To rest the weary and to soothe the sad,
> Doth lesson happier men, and shames at least the bad.

Over another feast cooked by Ylli of soup and pasta, we discussed our plans – still being watched attentively by the film crews. We were all, especially the horses, tired by now. The going on the last stretch had been harder than I had anticipated – or than it had looked on the recce when, from the valley below, I had seen the string of villages dotted along the mountainside and imagined riding between them. We had reached the Byron Trail, which had always been our objective, and there seemed little point in killing

ourselves to reach the Greek border. So I proposed that we take it easy for
the last few days and instead of spending whole days riding, take some time
to let Mickey get some good film. It also seemed only polite, since so many
of them had turned out to see us, to allow the Albanian press corps a chance
to film us. This decision seemed to please everyone, although perhaps Auron
was a little disappointed that we were not going to follow the whole Byron
Trail, and so further his ambition to promote it as a major tourist attraction.

Darkness fell and from out of the night came herds of silky goats and
shaggy sheep being driven home from pasture. Behind them, looming out
of the darkness, ambled a herd of cows, their deeper bells lulling us to sleep.
Throughout the night dogs barked all around, but we were far too weary
to notice.

The next morning was set aside for Mickey to film. While he did so, the
Albanian film crews either filmed as well or, when Mickey didn't need us,
interviewed us on various topics. On the way into Terbuq we had passed a
picturesque dell with gnarled trees and rugged rocks. I suggested it would
make a good background for some of the pieces he wanted us to do to
camera. I sat on a rock and Mickey asked me to talk about Byron. Without
being at all sure of my facts, I spoke on the origins of the romantic movement, asserting confidently that it all started at that very spot, whose wild,
brooding landscape spawned the idyllic myth. I continued, a little carried
away: as Byron and Hobhouse had passed, almost exactly 200 years before,
I suggested that Byron had been inspired by this scene to start *Childe Harold*.
'*Childe*' was the medieval word for a young candidate for knighthood. Its
central character was the first hero of the romantic movement, moody, intro-
spective, a loner, and he was to be the model for many to follow, the most
recent of which has been, perhaps, Harry Potter. Of course it was nonsense,
as they may well not have passed that way and if they had it would have
looked very different, but I enjoyed doing it. Later I learned of another
similarity between those two heroes. Two months before, there had been
scenes unprecedented in modern times when the latest Harry Potter book
had been published. People had queued for hours, even days, to get copies

and the literary world was gripped with an almost hysterical frenzy. On *Childe Harold's* publication day John Murray's offices in Albemarle Street were besieged by mobs demanding copies. The situation became so tense that the publisher had to resort to throwing copies out of the windows into the crowd below. Twenty thousand copies were sold on that one day and, as Byron said, he 'awoke one morning to find himself famous'.

One of the Albanian film directors, who had been quietly watching, started quoting a poem. It was in Albanian, but I recognised the words *'Tambourgi! Tambourgi!'*, which are the memorable opening lines of a *Childe Harold* stanza:

> Tambourgi! Tambourgi! Thy larum afar
> Gives hope to the valiant, and promise of war;
> All the sons of the mountains arise at the note,
> Chimariot, Illyrian and dark Suliote!"

The director's name was Artan Rama and he told me that he had learned a lot of the poem at school and never forgotten it. How many English people could recite Byron today, I wondered; in this part of the world he is revered as a great hero and a proponent of liberty. It is well known that he died of a fever at Mesolonghi fighting for Greek independence, less so that he is such a hero in Albania. As we have seen, national independence was not an issue when he was there, but he influenced succeeding generations as a symbol of rebellion, adventure and romance. Not only was he the first to fire the West's imagination with the romance of Albania through his poetry but, in an indirect way, he could also be said to be partly responsible for Albania's independence today. It is a curious story. In 1809, Byron bought a traditional Albanian costume in Janina, a town that is now in Greece but which was then considered part of Albania. The costume was made of an intricately embroidered gold and crimson velvet jacket worn over a heavily gilded short waistcoat and with a colourful blue, green and red shawl wound round the head. It was in this extravagant attire that Byron was painted in

1813 by the fashionable portrait painter Thomas Phillips. One of the best-known portraits of Byron, it was exhibited at the Royal Academy and now hangs in the British Embassy in Athens. Phillips later painted two further copies of the portrait. One is on permanent display in the National Portrait Gallery in London – one of the most popular portraits there – and the other, commissioned by John Murray, Byron's publishers, hangs in their offices in Albemarle Street. While the picture was being painted, Byron was carrying on a correspondence – and perhaps a flirtation – with an extremely rich Scottish heiress called Margaret Mercer Elphinstone. Known as 'the fops' despair', she was a great coquette, but also an independent woman and the same age as Byron. On 3 May 1814, he sent her his Albanian costume to wear as fancy dress. In the accompanying letter he wrote, 'If you like the dress – keep it. I shall be very glad to get rid of it – as it reminds me of one or two things I don't want to remember . . . I have worn this very little, and never in England except for half an hour to Phillips. It will do for a masquerade.' I would love to know what it was that he was trying to forget, but history does not relate.

Margaret Mercer was to be the only one who stood by Byron to the last, when all his friends and acquaintances had turned their backs on him, a response to rumours of incest, sodomy and adultery. In his final letter to Margaret, which he wrote from Dover as he left England in disgrace, never to return, he sent her this message via a friend: 'Tell her that had I been fortunate enough to marry a woman like her, I should not now be obliged to exile myself from my country.'

Byron's Albanian costume now hangs in Bowood House, the home of the 4th Marquess of Lansdowne, who married Margaret Mercer's eldest daughter. I like to imagine Mercer's grandchildren playing with it when they were young. Perhaps they asked their grandmother about this exotic piece in their home and perhaps she told them, with a twinkle in her eye, about how she had known Lord Byron and that it came from a wild and beautiful country that had enchanted him.

Many years later, in 1880, the younger son, Lord Edmond Fitzmaurice, became a member of a boundary commission in the Balkans and was the very first person to propose a united Albania. This was some time before the Albanians started agitating for independence themselves and as a result he, too, is regarded as a hero in that country. I like to think that it was the childhood influence of the costume, his grandmother's stories and *Childe Harold*, which he must have read and probably learned by heart, which led him to want freedom for Albania.

On our return from Albania, I was able to persuade the present Lord Lansdowne, great-great-grandson of Miss Mercer and great-nephew of Lord Edmond, to pose beside the costume and tell some of this story.

However inaccurate and fanciful my spontaneous history of the romantic movement might have been, there is no doubt that it was Byron who, through *Childe Harold*, set Albania firmly in nineteenth-century consciousness as one of the most romantic places in the world. 'The wild Albanian kirtled to his knee/ With shawl-girt head and ornamented gun/ And gold-embroidered garments, fair to see . . . ' became the image of a fierce yet generous people fighting for independence, hated by Turks and Greeks alike.

Byron described Albanian dress as 'the most wonderful in the world'. Another British traveller, John Fraser, who rode throughout the country at the turn of the twentieth century, wrote

> . . . the Albanian struck me as something of a dandy. He loves his jacket to be braided with silver and gold. His kilt is usually spotlessly clean. His shoes, often of red leather, have a huge puff-ball on each toe, which did not strike me as beautiful, but which the Albanian himself thinks particularly 'Swagger.' The brace of revolvers carried at his waist are invariably carved and inlaid, whilst if he prefers a gun it is long and slender and also carved and inlaid, often with precious stones, with an inset gold inscription running along the barrel.

Today, as a result of poverty, communism, the usual influences from the West, men and women alike wear the same dreary clothes as the rest of us:

jeans, jackets, open shirts. But in the remoter hill villages we had been riding through, we had seen traces of what went before. In the north some old men still wore the white skull cap of their Islamic faith; and in the mountains of central Albania the women often wore full-length baggy shalwar trousers, but we seldom saw signs of the style and flamboyance which must have been such a feature of dress in Byron's day.

Byron's faithful Italian servant, Giovanni Battista Falcieri, who was with him when he died at Mesolonghi, had come into his employ first as his gondolier in Venice. Shelley, for whom he also worked for a time, described him in a letter from Ravenna: 'Tita, the Venetian, is here, and operates as my valet – a fine fellow with a prodigious black beard who has stabbed two or three people, and who is the most good-natured looking fellow I ever saw.' Byron introduces him in *Don Juan* (II.56) with what must be the worst couplet in the poem:

> Battista, though (a name call'd shortly Tita)
> Was lost by getting at some aqua-vita

After the poet's death, Tita fought for the Greek cause at the head of a regiment of Albanians, with whom he must have felt quite at home. A few years later, he was picked up by Disraeli and his companion, Clay, destitute in Malta and eventually sent as a servant to Disraeli's father Isaac D'Israeli, who had been a friend of Byron's, at his country house, Bradenham, in rural Buckinghamshire. There he caused a stir similar to that created by Aubrey Herbert's Kiazim in the next century, with his peculiar dress and habits, but he married the English housekeeper and became a favourite of the old man, who eventually died in his arms.

Our day passed pleasantly as, for once, there was no pressure on us and we could chat with the charming journalists who had come a long way to be with us. We put the horses to graze on the lush grass in the churchyard next to our camp while Ylli prepared a picnic lunch for us and all the film crews. We also spoke to Prince Leka, urging him to try to come to Tepelenë in two days, where we planned to film in Ali Pasha's castle, once the centre of his opulent court, the epitome of Oriental luxury and hedonism. It is a huge fortress, which he had built by European engineers when at the height of his power. After all, Ali Pasha had been offered the crown of Albania a hundred years before Leka's own grandfather became the first king. But sadly, he couldn't make it.

On the way to Labovë, the film crews still following and filming, we passed a substantial church being built and were told that it was to be a monastery. As the afternoon wore on and became hot we found a beautiful ruined stone building, blanketed in a huge creeper. We spent the rest of the afternoon in its cool, dark shade and stayed to camp there that night.

I enjoy being interviewed without rehearsal or any idea what I am about to be asked. I find that my brain works best when put on the spot by the unexpected and it is fun having to think on my feet while the camera or tape is running. There is a peculiar freedom, too, in doing this abroad, where my peers are unlikely ever to know what I have said and thus make fun of my foolishness.

As we sat talking to the film crews, one interviewer asked me, 'What did you discover in Albania, as an explorer?' I replied, 'An explorer doesn't just discover things. An explorer tries to change the world. I hope to change the global perception of Albania.'

Another asked how I could reconcile encouraging tourism to the more remote regions of the country with the danger that it would undermine and destroy traditional hospitality where taking payment was unthinkable. I replied that I agreed it was probably impossible, but that developing a reputation for exceptionally generous hotel service, welcoming guests with open-handed liberality might achieve the best of both worlds.

Albania's aspiration to join the EU was often brought up. Negotiations are already well in hand and EU officials have set Albania's admission as a priority, although it is likely to take a long time before criteria for economic and political stability are met. Currently, Albania is down as among the last 'potential candidate countries', but in the case of Albania I would hesitate before agreeing that their joining the EU would be a good thing. A people's sense of uniqueness is their most valuable asset and nowhere is this truer than in Albania. People, whether they are a remote Amazonian tribe like the Yanomami, or the descendants of an ancient culture like the Khmer in Cambodia, believe that they are singular, and therefore perhaps superior, in some way. Despite their long and tragic history of occupation and subjugation, Albanians have retained an intense pride in themselves and their believed greatness; this extends through village, clan and national levels and every Albanian feels it. Their dream to be incorporated into the EU is understandable, as many face grinding poverty in the wake of communism, but I believe it would be a mistake for the country to be 'rescued' in this way. It would undermine so much that is special about Albania. A nation that chooses to join the EU from a position of reasonable stability and strength may prosper. But a country that joins from a belief that this will solve its problems and perhaps also with a lingering sense of despair, has every chance of destroying itself.

It was very good to be able to talk to intelligent people who spoke good English. The journalists drifted away to drive back into Tepelenë or Gjirokastër, but Auron stayed and we could pick his brains about local history. Many diverse people are associated with Labovë. An exotic brigand called Christos Hadji-Petros, who was to become the 'scandalous' Jane Digby's lover, was one. In 1852 Hadji-Petros was the head of a group of feared Albanian mercenaries, the Palikares, who had fought valorously in the Greek War of Independence twenty-eight years earlier (in which Byron had died). With nothing much to do after the war, they had turned to brigandage and terrorised the Greek countryside. Travellers were liable to be stripped of all they had and left to walk naked into the nearest town. The first king of Greece, Otto I, whose father King Ludwig I of Bavaria (grandfather of the mad one) had been another of Jane Digby's lovers, decided to turn the 'poacher' – perhaps in the hope that a solid job would deter him from further crimes – into a 'gamekeeper' and made him the King's General and Governor of Albania. His extraordinarily ironic brief was to make the roads of his country safe. Jane Digby rode with Hadji-Petros and his band of Palikares, sleeping in caves and under the stars, shooting partridges from the saddle, making love and swearing eternal fidelity. The relationship ended when he started an affair with her devoted French maid of thirteen years, Eugénie. Digby sailed for Syria, taking Eugénie with her, since she considered that men were easier to come by than a good maid.

Perhaps the most illustrious of Labovë's sons was Evangelis Zappas, born there in 1800. After serving as a mercenary soldier in Ali Pasha's army, he went to Wallachia, now part of Romania, and became one of the richest men in Eastern Europe. He used his fortune to finance a permanent revival of the ancient Olympic Games, with the first modern and international event taking place in 1859, in Athens. When he died in 1865, he left his vast fortune for the modern Olympic Games to be held every four years. Some of the money went to build a stadium called the Zappeion, which was used in both the 1896 Athens Olympic Games, the first under the IOC, and the 2004 Athens Games.

That night, we built a big bonfire of driftwood we had collected from around the ruins and sat around its warm glow drinking raki, while Auron told us stories and I read extracts from *Childe Harold*. A local shepherd, who had brought us armfuls of good hay for the horses, came to sit and talk as well. For once, thanks to Auron, we could converse properly with a local. I asked him how things were under communism. 'Oh, those times were much better!' he said, enthusiastically. 'The village was alive then. We had a proper hospital, there was electricity all day and night and the postal service worked – not like now. And we had a cultural centre with lots of parties. We were one big family with a proper sense of community and we felt quite safe. A woman could walk home in the dark without fear. Even down in Tepelenë there was only one policeman. Now there are many. Of course it was a repressive regime, but everything worked and we cared for our country. There was no rubbish anywhere and no fires in the forests. We planted trees everywhere. Now it is hard.' He gazed into the fire thinking back to the happy times he remembered, and we all went silent and thoughtful for a bit too. Then the raki was passed round again and we cheered up. For the first time, even Durim, who had been sulking all day for a reason that even Auron could not fathom, became animated and said something nice about us, if faintly enigmatic. 'These people have come to our country to make things better. Perhaps they will bring back the good old days.'

Chapter 15

Sporting Brits and Cruel Pashas

'The Albanians in general . . . have a fine cast of countenance; and the most beautiful women I ever beheld, in stature and in features, we saw levelling the road broken down by the torrents . . .'
Byron's notes to *Childe Harold*

As we were enjoying a leisurely breakfast our shepherd friend arrived with more hay and joined us for coffee. He said that his brother would accompany us that day, so that we did not get lost as the way ahead was not simple. This was the first time such an offer had been made and I wondered where we had gone wrong. The answer was probably that Auron had explained to everyone in the village exactly what we were doing and why, and this had triggered the innate Albanian desire to help a stranger.

With the shepherd came an overexcited chestnut stallion, which was only interested in stealing the hay and making advances to Bora. The local way of dealing with such things was to throw stones, which would drive it away for a while, until it sneaked back. There is a wonderful clip in one of the videos Mickey made at this time of Louella talking seriously to camera about mules, when the stallion appears in the background, unknown to her, pursued by a furious woman chucking rocks at it until they exit stage left. It looks uncannily like a scene from *Borat*.

The way to our final destination, Erind, was indeed difficult, and we would certainly have been lost without the shepherd's brother. We had decided to finish the ride there as it had good access from the main road running along the valley for a truck to collect the horses, and Hobhouse describes sleeping there in a comfortable Turkish house. Our guide took us far up into the hills to avoid the ravines running across our route and we were rewarded with fine views across the valley toward Gjirokastër, the beautiful old town with a fine castle on the far side of the Drino River. At the highest point we found a little ruined church with a small track, the high road back to Terbuq, curling round to the left. We had seen no one for an hour, but at that precise moment a figure sitting sidesaddle on a white horse came trotting up. It was our good friend from Terbuq who had lavished us with grapes and hay. We greeted each other happily. He told the shepherd's brother to go home as he would now look after us since he too was heading for Erind. Dressed in a smart suit and new black shoes, we guessed he was off to see his girlfriend. As he led us up and down almost invisible tracks he chatted away merrily in Albanian, to which we replied in English. Somehow, we seemed to understand each other perfectly and our exchanges were accompanied by much laughter. Once we were able to look down on the village of Erind and, far below, the flat ground where we would make our last camp and finish our journey, we both felt a wave of relief tinged with sadness flood over us. In spite of all the unexpected difficulties, we had done it and not only that: we had survived storm and tempest to see some of the most thrilling mountainous countryside in Europe, met unusual people, many still living in the Middle Ages: and we had done it together, spending many hours alone in the saddle, which is how we like to travel best.

A person who has inspired me most in my life was born in 1831 to a family not unlike mine in Ireland. Arthur Kavanagh travelled the world, largely by horse, at a time when it really was dangerous to do so, because there were footpads and bandits in those days who preyed on those who dared to roam. Kavanagh was a fearless hunter and an excellent shot. His servant developed frostbite in Persia and had to be sent home as he was in danger of losing all his toes; and both his eldest brother, Tom, and his tutor died along the way.

Kavanagh returned to Ireland from India, married, had a large family and became a distinguished Member of Parliament. In 1865, he sailed his yacht, the *Eva*, with some friends to Albania. He spent a month shooting woodcock, snipe and wild boar in the marshes and hills around the coast and rode into the interior. The remarkable thing about Arthur Kavanagh was that he had been born with virtually no arms and legs, just six-inch 'fins' which barely met across his broad chest and thighs. Nevertheless, he seemed to have also been born with an indomitable spirit of perseverance, which made him triumph over his physical defects and to ignore them, so that he learned to do almost all that a healthy man can do, but better. He was often carried on the back of a servant and he had an early wheelchair designed in which he was able to move about indoors. By long practice he made his stumps so supple and strong that, strapped on his horse in a special saddle, he could manage the reins as well as if he had them between fingers, and he even made good use of a whip. He was an expert angler, fishing from a boat or from horseback. When shooting, he carried his gun without a trigger-guard, resting it on his left arm and jerking the trigger with his right. He also became a competent draughtsman and painter and wrote more legibly than many who suffer from no physical defect. Perhaps the thing I admire most about him was the way that he almost never referred to his appalling disability but instead, through sheer force of personality, rose above it and made all around him do the same.

When the going became rough in Albania, when we were struggling at the end of a long day in the saddle, when my horse would not do what I wanted it to do, when danger threatened, I would think of Arthur Kavanagh and my petty problems would fade into insignificance.

We had arranged by telephone with our trusty horse-transporter in Elbasan, Bujar Dishani, to collect the horses the next day from the road below Erind. He was to take them first to Tepelenë, where we wanted to do some more filming, then he was to return Semi to Arjan Rugji at Pezë before driving back to Elbasan with Bora.

After saying goodbye to our laughing friend from Terbuq, we stopped under a spreading maple tree beside the road, where a shepherd was tending his flock of what Louella described as 'biblical sheep'. Huddled in a tight group with their heads together in the centre they looked as though they were praying; some of the time they were motionless, conserving their energies as the sun beat down on them; when they moved, they moved all together, like a rugby scrum. We waited in the shade until Auron joined us, bringing Tirana's main daily newspaper with him. There was a picture of us on the front page and a long article inside. He told us that we had already been on national television the night before and further programmes were planned. We basked happily in our new-found fame, even though we wished it had come at the start, rather than the end, of our journey.

That evening, Louella cleaned and polished the Western saddle she had been lent, and which we had had repaired, and wrote to Bora's owner, Tony, and his sister, who would translate it for him:

Dear Tony and Roseta,

Firstly thank you, from the bottom of my heart, for letting us take Bora on this big adventure with us. I wish she could talk to you as I think she would tell you many things.

She would tell you first of all that we loved her and were very kind to her. She was very kind and loving to us. I rode her carefully, never had a stick, and was very gentle with her mouth. We had to walk and lead the horses for probably half of our journey. Bora is so strong that I could not lead her, so I just hooked her reins on the saddle and let her go. She just followed on her own, and when we climbed steep hills she let me hold on to her tail and she pulled me up the hill. She is a wonderful horse!

She is also very brave and strong. She has crossed rivers, she has climbed hills, she has walked fearlessly across wobbly suspension bridges, and had to go on horrible stony ground hour after hour. She never complained. She never gave up.

She had a great journey in her beautiful country and I am sure she enjoyed it and will remember it always.

So, thank you – I will miss her so much.

Louella

Early the next morning Bujar arrived, loaded the horses and drove them to Tepelenë. There was one more important scene we had to film before they and we went home. Ali Pasha was the reason Byron went to Albania just after coming down from Cambridge, and it was his descriptions of Ali Pasha's court that he found and stayed in which inspired some of his best poetry in *Childe Harold* and so scandalised London society. The shocking images of the licentious East, which Byron was to turn into thrilling poetry, were described more prosaically and accurately by his companion Hobhouse:

every thing . . . was presently forgotten, when we entered through the gateway in a tower, and found ourselves in the court-yard of the Vizier's palace.

The court at Tepellene, which was enclosed on two sides by the palace, and on the other two sides by a high wall, presented us, at our first entrance, with a sight something like what we might have, perhaps, beheld some hundred years ago in the castle-yard of a great Feudal Lord. Soldiers, with their arms piled against the wall near them, were assembled in different parts of the square: some of them pacing slowly backwards and forwards, and others sitting on the ground in groups. Several horses, completely caparisoned, were leading about, whilst others were neighing under the hands of the grooms. In the part farthest from the dwelling, preparations were making for the feast of the night; several kids and sheep were being dressed by cooks who were themselves half armed. Everything wore a most martial look, though not exactly in the style of the head-quarters of a Christian general.

He describes Ali Pasha as having a full white beard and an imperious eye:

. . . a short man, about five feet five inches in height, and very fat . . . his high turban, composed of many small rolls, seemed of fine gold muslin, and his attaghan, or long dagger, was studded with brilliants . . . Ali indulges to the full in all the pleasures that are licensed by the custom of the country. His harem is said to contain three hundred women. His other gratifications cannot be very varied or refined . . . the court fool, who was distinguished by a very high round cap of fur; but unlike the ancient fools of more civilised monarchs, this fellow is obliged to confine his humour to gambolling, cutting capers, and tumbling before the Vizier's horse, when his Highness takes a ride.

Byron's description of the same scene in *Childe Harold* is more colourful:

Richly caparisoned, a ready row
Of armed horse, and many a warlike store,
Circled the wide extending court below:
Above, strange groups adorned the corridore:
And oft-times through the Area's echoing door,
Some high-capped Tartar spurred his steed away:
The Turk, the Greek, the Albanian, and the Moor,
Here mingled in their many-hued array,
While the deep war-drum's sound announced the close of day.

The wild Albanian kirtled to his knee,
With shawl-girt head and ornamented gun,
And gold-embroidered garments fair to see;
The crimson-scarfed men of Macedon;
The Delhi with his cap of terror on,
And crooked glaive; the lively, supple Greek;
And swarthy Nubia's mutilated son;
The bearded Turk that rarely deigns to speak,
Master of all around, too potent to be meek,
Are mixed conspicuous; some recline in groups,
Scanning the motley scene that varies round;

In his letters home to his mother, Byron describes how Ali flirted with him; he wrote that Ali admired his 'small ears, curling hair, and little white hands . . . he treated me like a child, sending me almonds & sugared sherbet, fruit and sweetmeats twenty times a day. He begged me to visit him "often, and at night, when he was more at leisure".' The suggestion that Byron reciprocated these advances helped to build the aura of scandal about *Childe Harold*. Although unlikely, the rumours were further exacerbated by Byron giving as one motive for his journey through Albania the desire to write a treatise, 'to be entitled "Sodomy simplified or Pæderasty proved to be praiseworthy from ancient authors and from modern practice".' A stanza shortly after the one above originally read:

> Here woman's voice is never heard – apart,
> And scarce permitted guarded, veiled to move,
> She yields to one her person and her heart,
> Tamed to her cage, nor feels a wish to rove;
> For boyish minions of unhallowed love
> The shameless torch of wild desire is lit,
> Caressed, preferred even woman's self above,
> Whose forms for Nature's gentler errors fit
> All frailties mote excuse save that which they commit.

On the advice of his friends, Byron changed the second part of the printed version to the innocuous:

> Tamed to her cage, nor feels a wish to rove;
> For, not unhappy in her master's love,
> And joyful in a mother's gentlest cares,
> Blest care! All other feelings far above!
> Herself more sweetly rears the babe she bears,
> Who never quits the breast, no meaner passion shares.

Edward Lear reached Tepelenë fifty years after Byron and found it much changed: 'a dreary, blank scene of desolation, where once, and so recently, was all the rude magnificence of Oriental despotism!' He had looked forward to seeing for himself the 'pomp' described by both the earlier travellers, writing that, 'of all days passed in Albania, this has most keenly interested me', but he was disappointed. The *khan* or inn where he stayed was 'a concatenation of minute cells or closets, with uncloseable doors, pervious to cats and dogs, while a perverse old goat with a bell round his neck, who infests the wooden gallery, bumps and jingles up and down it all night long'.

Below the walls of Ali Pasha's castle the Vjosë River, now joined by the Drino, was described by Hobhouse as being 'as broad as the Thames at Westminster Bridge'. Here the piers of what, according to Auron, had once been a fine bridge built for Ali Pasha by a Frenchman, now supported a long and perilous suspension bridge. Mickey had decided that a suitable finale to his film would be a shot of us riding across to the castle. This Byron and Hobhouse didn't actually do, as they had already crossed to the left bank by a long-vanished bridge across the Drino and in their day the bridge probably hadn't even been built anyway, but this did not deter Mickey's artistic enthusiasm. The horses were unloaded again and we led them down the narrow track along the side of the precipice above the river to the point where the bridge was anchored.

We had to wait for some time as first a hunter with his gun over his shoulder and his good-looking hounds went across. He was followed by a woman and some children leading a mule. We did not want to have to pass anyone on the bridge and it was some time before the whole 300 or so metres were unimpeded. We set off, leading Semi in front, with Bora behind. It was far worse than it looked. From the moment we set foot on the first span everything swayed and shook. It was so bad that Louella and I had trouble staying upright and we had to clutch the suspension cable to keep our balance. The rushing water was a long way below us and there was little to stop a horse falling to its death if things went badly wrong. There was no turning back and we crept on, sweating with fear. As we neared the far bank Bora stepped on a loose plank which flipped up and she fell over, her legs flailing. I looked back and for a ghastly moment thought that both she and Louella, who was hanging on to her, would roll over the side and drop to the rocks beneath. But neither of them panicked, as I suspect I would have, and to the accompaniment of Louella's soothing instructions Bora regained her feet. 'Mickey,' I said, in my last call to him over our Albanian mobile phones, 'there is no way we are riding back over this bridge. You will just have to make do with us leading them again – and that may well end in disaster. Oh, and there is no way we will do it again if you don't get it right first time!'

We waited while another group of schoolchildren first petted the horses and then skipped merrily across the bridge. Then we had to go back, this time knowing we were being filmed. I can't remember an occasion when my heart has been in my mouth for quite so long. The wind had got up, making the bridge sway sickeningly. As we crossed each pier, we could see how it moved a good metre from side to side and at one point I was within an ace of falling over. Soldiers are trained to 'break step' when crossing swing bridges, but you can't make a horse do this. On the last span, the longest, everything started bucking up and down alarmingly; there was nothing we could do but keep going and, at last, it was over.

Once we were back up with the lorry, things happened in a too-quick blur. One moment we were kissing our good horses goodbye – then they were loaded and gone. Louella and I, tears streaming down our faces, watched the lorry until it was out of sight.

pot of Europe, where races and creeds have mingled and, from time to time, massacred each other. Yet throughout these conflicts, these indomitable peoples of so many ethnic origins, languages, creeds and ideologies have forged on with their lives. Whenever there have been periods of peace, they have built houses and cultivated their land. The evidence is all around to see. Successive waves of disaster have destroyed them but, again and again, they rise phoenix-like from the ashes.

A revival is what is happening now in Albania and it is inspiring to see. The old have stayed in Albania to keep the home-fires burning; the young have gone abroad to seek their fortunes. This is something Albanians have always done, since long before they had a country of their own. Under the Turks, they served their masters so well that they took over many of the most important roles in running the Ottoman Empire. Later they were to become acclaimed mercenaries, fighting all over the world. And they often settled abroad to found new Albanian communities. Since communism, they have begun travelling again, this time to the USA and elsewhere in Europe. But their homeland is still and will always be Albania and many dream of returning, in spite of the difficulties. Some are coming home and undoubtedly over the years more will join them. All they need is a little peace and, perhaps, a little help to make Albania a stable and prosperous country again.

The mountains between the fertile Drino and Vjosë valleys and the sea look from below as bare as an elephant's back, but once over them the gorges running down to the Adriatic coast are as lush as anywhere around the whole of the Mediterranean. They lead to some of the most dramatic and unspoilt coastal scenery left along either coast of the Adriatic but this is rapidly being threatened by the sort of development of which the Minister of Tourism would heartily approve. Perhaps the only benefit from Albania's isolation and poverty under communism was a coastline that was left untouched by mass tourism and its ugly trappings. Now much of it is dusty with urgent lorries and other heavy machinery building high-rise hotels and neon-lit restaurants. It will take time to destroy it all, but every effort seems to be under way to do so. Further north, near Durres, huge concrete towers of high-rise apartments block out all views of the sea from the road and all the original semi-tropical vegetation has been bulldozed aside. Everyone knows that these constructions are funded by local, Kosovan and even foreign Mafia money.

We saw a side of Albania few are privileged to see and it touched us. We were lucky to do so before whatever changes lie ahead come to pass. The story of Albania is a sad one, but never dull. There are reputed to be three Chinese curses of increasing severity: 'May you live in interesting times'; 'May you come to the attention of those in authority'; and 'May you find what you are looking for'. It is my wish for Albania that they suffer none of these. Far from being catapulted into a chaotic world, for which they are ill prepared, Albanians deserve now a period of peace and stability after all the turmoil they have been through. Their strength comes from the very spirit of independence and sheer bloody-mindedness, what Ismail Kadare called their 'crackpottedness', which makes them so different. It is this that maintains their fierce individuality and their obsessive hospitality. We should recognise that difference and reward them for it; if we do we will find that not only they, but we, are richer for it.

Select Bibliography

Allcock, John and Young, Antonia: *Black Lambs and Grey Falcons*. 1991. Bradford Univ Press

Amery, Julian: *Sons of the Eagle*. 1948. Macmillan

Bailey, Roderick: *The Wildest Province: SOE in the Land of the Eagle*. 2008. Jonathan Cape

Best, Captain J.: *Excursions in Albania*. 1842. Wm. H. Allen & Co.

Bethell, Nicholas: *The Great Betrayal*. 1984. Hodder & Stoughton

Buchan, John: *Greenmantle*. 1916. Hodder & Stoughton

Byron, Lord: *Childe Harold's Pilgrimage*. 1812. John Murray

Carver, Robert: *The Accursed Mountains*. 1998. John Murray

Cohen, David: *Kavanagh MP: An Inspirational Story*. 2005. Psychology News Press

Davies, Edmund 'Trotsky': *Illyrian Venture*. 1952. The Bodley Head

De Waal, Clarissa: *Albania Today*. 2005. I.B.Tauris

Disraeli, Benjamin (Earl of Beaconsfield): *The Rise of Iskander*. 1906. John Lane

Durham, M. Edith: *High Albania*. 1985. Virago Press/Some Tribal Origins, Laws and Customs of the Balkans. 1928. Allen & Unwin/Twenty Years of Balkan Tangle. 1920. George Allen & Unwin/Albania and The Albanians. 2001. Centre for Albanian Studies

Elsie, Robert: *An Elusive Eagle Soars: Anthology of Modern Albanian Poetry*. 1993. UNESCO/Forest

Faber, David: *Speaking for England*. 2005. The Free Press

Fielding, Xan: *One Man in his Time*. 1990. Macmillan

Gloyer, Gillian: *The Bradt Guide to Albania*. 2006. Bradt Travel Guides

Gordon, Jan and Cora: *Two Vagabonds in Albania*. 1927. The Bodley Head

Hasluck, Margaret: *The Unwritten Law in Albania*. 1954. Cambridge Univ Press

Heaton-Armstrong, Duncan: *The Six Month Kingdom*. 2005. I.B.Tauris

Herbert, Aubrey: *Ben Kendim: a Record of Eastern Travel*. 1924, Hutchinson

Hobhouse, John (Lord Broughton): *A Journey through Albania*. 1855. John Murray

Hoxha, Enver: *The Anglo-American Threat to Albania*. 1982. The Institute of Marxist-Leninist Studies at the Central Committee of the Party of Labour of Albania

Hudhri, Ferid: *Albania through Art*. 2003. Onufri/Albania and Albanians in World Art. 1990. Christos Giovanis. Athens

Hyman, Susan: *Edward Lear in the Levant*. 1988. John Murray

Kadare, Ismail: *Broken April*. 1991. Harper Collins/Chronicle in Stone. 1987. Serpent's Tail/Albanian Spring. 1995. Saqi Books/The Successor. 2006. Canongate/The File on H. 1998. Arcade Publishing Inc.

Kemp, Peter: *No Colours or Crest*. 1958. Cassell & Co.

Knight, Edward: *Albania. A Narrative of Recent Travel*. 1880. Sampson Low & Co.

Leake, W.M.: *Travels in the Morea*. 1830. John Murray

Lear, Edward: *Journals of a Landscape Painter in the Balkans*. 1988. Century

Malcolm, Noel: *Kosovo: A Short History*. 1998. Papermac

McCormick, Donald: *The Incredible Mr Kavanagh*. 1960. Putnam

Minta, Stephen: *On a Voiceless Shore: Byron in Greece*. 1998. Henry Holt & Co.

Newby, Eric: *On the Shores of the Mediterranean*. 1984. Harvill Press

O'Sullivan, Firmin: *The Egnatian Way*. 1972. David & Charles

Oakley-Hill, D.R.: *An Englishman in Albania*. 2002. The Centre for Albanian Studies

Pearson, Owen: *Albania in the Twentieth Century: A History. 3 Volumes*. 2004-6. The Centre for Albanian Studies, in association with I.B.Tauris

Pettifer, James: *Albania and Kosovo Blue Guide*. 1996. A & C Black

Quayle, Anthony: *Eight Hours from England*. 1945. William Heinemann

Robyns, Gwen: *Geraldine of the Albanians*. 1987. Muller, Blond & White

Smiley, David: *Albanian Assignment*. 1985. Sphere Books

Sterling, Col. W.F.: *Safety Last*. 1953. Hollis & Carter

Strangford, Viscountess: *The Eastern Shores of the Adriatic in 1863*. 1864. Richard Bentley

Swire, Joseph: *Albania: The Rise of a Kingdom*. 1929. Williams & Norgate/ King Zog's Albania. 1937. Robert Hale

Tilman, H.W.: *When Men and Mountains Meet*. 1946. Cambridge Univ Press

Vickers, Miranda: *The Albanians – A modern History*. 2006. I.B.Tauris

Wilder, Rose Lane: *The Peaks of Shala*. 1923. Harper & Brothers

Young, Antonia: *Women who Become Men: Albanian Sworn Virgins*. 2000. Berg

Index

Index

Index